courageous
kindness

More books by (in)courage

Take Heart: 100 Devotions to Seeing God When Life's Not Okay

The Simple Difference:
How Every Small Kindness Makes a Big Impact

LOOK FOR OTHER TITLES IN THIS SERIES:

Courageous Simplicity:
Abide in the Simple Abundance of Jesus

Courageous Joy:
Delight in God through Every Season

Courageous Influence:
Embrace the Way God Made You for Impact

Courageous Kindness:
Live the Simple Difference Right Where You Are

For more resources, visit incourage.me.

AN
(in)courage
BIBLE STUDY

courageous kindness

LIVE THE SIMPLE DIFFERENCE RIGHT WHERE YOU ARE

Written by Becky Keife
and the (in)courage Community

Revell

a division of Baker Publishing Group
Grand Rapids, Michigan

Published by Revell
a division of Baker Publishing Group
PO Box 6287, Grand Rapids, MI 49516-6287
www.revellbooks.com

Printed in the United States of America

Library of Congress Cataloging-in-Publication Data
Title: Courageous kindness : live the simple difference right where you are.
Description: Grand Rapids, Michigan : Revell, a division of Baker Publishing Group, [2021] | "An (in)courage Bible study." | Includes bibliographical references.
Identifiers: LCCN 2021003935 | ISBN 9780800738068 (paperback) | ISBN 9781493431854 (ebook)
Subjects: LCSH: Kindness—Religious aspects—Christianity—Textbooks. | Influence (Psychology)—Religious aspects—Christianity—Textbooks. | Change—Religious aspects—Christianity—Textbooks.
Classification: LCC BV4647.K5 C68 2021 | DDC 241/.4—dc23
LC record available at https://lccn.loc.gov/2021003935

(in)courage is represented by Alive Literary Agency, www.aliveliterary .com.

In keeping with biblical principles of creation stewardship, Baker Publishing Group advocates the responsible use of our natural resources. As a member of the Green Press Initiative, our company uses recycled paper when possible. The text paper of this book is composed in part of post-consumer waste.

21 22 23 24 25 26 27   7 6 5 4 3 2 1

contents

introduction

Have you ever looked at the world's limitless problems in comparison with your limited resources and wondered if it's even possible for one person to make a meaningful difference? Or maybe you think about today's culture and feel disheartened by all the critical voices and division. Maybe kindness seems like a long-lost virtue without enough power to impact a single life let alone change the world. If thoughts like these swirl through your mind as you pick up a Bible study called *Courageous Kindness*, you're not alone.

The good news is that you don't have to come to this study with all your doubts resolved. You don't have to already know what it means to be courageously kind. All you need is a willingness to show up with an open heart and let God share His heartbeat with you.

Through the pages of Scripture and stories from women just like you, we'll discover how God's kindness is an unrelenting pursuit of human hearts *and* an invitation to partner with Him.

God is absolutely wild about people—including *you*! His kindness is the catalyst for our salvation; His work in our lives is like a love letter inviting others to repentance and relationship. Throughout this study, we'll see how God goes to unimaginable lengths to wow and woo and call His children to Himself. Does this mean life is easy, peachy, and pain-free? We all know the answer to that is a resounding no. Yet when we learn to live with eyes wide open to the evidence of God's kindness, it will not only change our view and understanding of God but will transform the way we see and relate to others.

How we treat people at work and church, how we love our kids and help a neighbor, how we give what we have even when it feels painfully insufficient—these things matter. God wants to use your ordinary days—as you go on your way—to accomplish more than you could ever expect.

Kindness is like stones being tossed in a pond. Each one of us will make temporary ripples when we obey God's call to be kind. But all of us together can create waves of lasting change in Jesus's name. *Courageous Kindness* is a journey unlike anything you've experienced. Let's dive in together.

How to Use This Study

If you found *Courageous Kindness* by reading *The Simple Difference* by Becky Keife, hooray! This study will help deepen your biblical understanding and life application of what it means for every small kindness to make a big impact. If you haven't read the book, no worries. This Bible study is complete on its own. But if you like *Courageous Kindness,* consider furthering your exploration of the topic by reading *The Simple Difference.*

Courageous Kindness is a great study for personal or small group use. If you're doing it with a group, we recommend allowing at least forty-five minutes for discussion, or more for larger groups. (We think groups of four to ten people work great!) Enhance your community study experience with our *Courageous Kindness* leader guide and videos. Go to www.incourage.me/leaderguides to download your small group resources. Whether you're an experienced small group leader or brand-new, we've got everything you need!

As you begin each day of this study, take a moment to be still and pray. Ask God to meet you, teach you, and convict you. Since there will be a lot of material to digest, take your time and feel free to go at your own pace.

Each week focuses on a different aspect of living with courageous kindness:

- **Week 1** encourages you to start right where you are—God's kindness is waiting for you.
- **Week 2** empowers you to use exactly what you have—even if it seems not enough.
- **Week 3** shows the power of bending low and lifting others up.
- **Week 4** equips you to put on compassion and embrace inconvenience.
- **Week 5** explores the impact of offering kindness for the long haul.
- **Week 6** shines a spotlight on God's ability to do more than you could expect.

Each week has a cadence that will help you get the most out of this study:

- **Day 1** looks at our call to courageously explore that week's theme.
- **Day 2** focuses on how Jesus lived out kindness and what we can learn from Him.
- **Day 3** addresses what the world says about that week's topic.
- **Day 4** shows us God's heart for us in the weekly topic.
- **Day 5** explores how we can become courageous women through each aspect of kindness.

We at (in)courage are excited to begin this *Courageous Kindness* journey with you. You'll see that each day opens with a story from one of our writers sharing her experience of offering or receiving kindness.

Our hope and prayer is that these stories will help you feel less alone and more inspired as you look for God in your own story.

Are you ready? Join us as we experience the radical kindness of God in fresh ways that will empower us to change the world—one simple, intentional act of kindness at a time.

right where you are

But God proves his own love for us in that while we
were still sinners, Christ died for us.

Romans 5:8

I did it again. My husband asked a simple question and I
became totally defensive. We were dishing up tacos for
dinner and he asked, "Is this all the carnitas?" And by those
five words he simply meant, "Is the pulled pork I see here
on the tray all there is, or do you have more in the oven?" It
wasn't a trick question. But what I *heard* was, "You should
have made more food. This is not enough. You failed."

See the chasm between his straightforward intention and my
assumption-laden perception?

I shot him a nasty look and in a rude tone answered, "Do you *see* any
more carnitas?"

He wanted to make sure he was divvying up the appropriate por-
tions between our sons' plates. I wanted to make sure my culinary
efforts were not criticized. Rather than checking myself and asking
my husband to clarify his simple question, I let sarcasm fly.

I felt threatened, and there was nothing kind about how I replied.

More often than I'd like to admit, I operate in relationships through a
lens of self-protectiveness. At its core, my defensiveness is a reflection
of one main thing: I doubt that I am loved for who I am. In other words,
I believe receiving love is dependent on what I do.

Yet I *know* this isn't true. My husband's love isn't conditional on how much carnitas I fix. And even more, God's love for me doesn't rely on anything I say or do. He loves me because I'm His daughter. Period.

My lack of assurance over how deeply I am loved has a direct impact on my ability to show love and kindness to others. *Ouch*. It's painful to confess that, but my taco-night tantrum makes it clear. However, I don't have to stay stuck in that defensive, sarcastic, painful place. Neither do you.

It takes courage to face the reality of false thinking. It takes courage to trust the kindness of God. To trust Him to rewire what we believe and how we behave so that we can reflect the truth of who He is and who we are as people made in His image. I've got a long way to go, but I'm ready to embark on this journey of courageous kindness.

—BECKY KEIFE

Is defensiveness ever your default reaction? How could intentionally remembering how much God loves you affect the way you respond to others?

This Bible study is about living with courageous kindness—making a simple difference by loving people in everyday ways as we go through life. We hope you're excited, because there's sweet revelation and world-changing transformation in store! But sometimes before we can focus on our next-step action, we need to come back to our firm foundation.

Everything we're going to talk about in this study hinges on this truth: "But God proves his own love for us in that while we were still sinners, Christ died for us" (Rom. 5:8).

The NIV translates the first part of this verse as, "God demonstrates his own love for us." God is putting all the evidence of His love clearly on display in the shocking, lavish, miraculous death and resurrection of Jesus. Because God loves us, He sent His own Son to die as the payment for all our sins. If you've been a Christian for a long time, this truth is probably ingrained in your spiritual DNA. But sometimes what is most familiar is most easily forgotten or overlooked.

It's time to get reacquainted with our awe of God's love.

We become accustomed to saying "God loves me" in the same breath as "I need another latte," and we allow both statements to hold the same weight over our day. It's easy to let our identity as God's children—sinners saved by grace, people loved and empowered by the mighty Creator—slip into the recesses of our mental sandbox.

Friend, *God loves you*! No matter what you did yesterday or when you were eighteen or how you'll blow it tomorrow. Whether you spend your days in a boardroom or a Lego-strewn living room, whether you're inputting data in a corner cubicle, serving as a barista at the corner coffee shop, or strolling with other seniors around the block—God loves you fully, completely, radically.

> **Let the reality of God's unconditional, no-limits, right-where-you-are love sink in deep. It's what changes everything.**

If you're new to reading the Bible, then *lean in here* all the more. Let the reality of God's unconditional, no-limits, right-where-you-are love sink in deep. It's what changes everything.

Look up John 1:12; Ephesians 2:4–5; and 1 John 3:1. What stands out to you from these verses? How else have you seen God demonstrate His love for you?

....

....

Read Romans 5:6–11. What do you think is the significance of Paul's back-to-back use of the phrase "how much more" (or simply "much more," depending on which translation you use)?

....

....

....

....

God's love is the foundation of His character and how He relates to people. Therefore, He always fills in our gaps with grace.

My opening story shows how I filled in the gap between my husband's words and my interpretation of them with judgment, sarcasm, and defensiveness. Not my finest moment. Sometimes it's so hard and messy to be human. Thankfully, God isn't human. We don't have to question His motives or second-guess His agenda. God isn't waiting to criticize what we've done or scrutinize our next move. God sees us through a lens of love. And He is kind to those He loves. Once we get this—a deep-in-our-bones, seeped-in-our-soul kind of *get* this—then we can live in surrendered trust that what God says is true and He has our best in mind.

First John 4:19 explains that "we love because he first loved us." We cannot love if we do not know, believe, and live like we are loved. The former hinges on the latter.

We'll bang this drum as loud and long as it takes. Don't tune out. *God loves you.* Today—in your marital stress or financial debt, in your broken friendship or chronic illness—God loves you. Breathe that in. It's not a throwaway Christian cliché or a trite Sunday school song lyric.

It's truth! God's love for His people is the main theme of humanity's story etched in Scripture, stretching from Genesis through Revelation. God's love and kindness are not dependent on people's performance. We all fail. Miserably.

He keeps on loving.

What keeps you from believing you are loved by God just as you are, right where you are?

Read Psalm 103:11–14 and Romans 8:38–39. How is God's love described? How have you seen this kind of persistent love and compassion displayed in your life?

So what do we do when we recognize that we have a hard time fully receiving God's love and showing it to others? Paul gives us a great starting point. He writes, "Do not be conformed to this age, but be transformed by the renewing of your mind, so you may discern what is the good, pleasing, and perfect will of God" (Rom. 12:2).

What's amazing is that God has already made His will known to us! Jesus boils it down by quoting Deuteronomy 6:5 and Leviticus 19:18:

"'Love the Lord your God with all your heart, with all your soul, and with all your mind.' This is the greatest and most important command. The second is like it: 'Love your neighbor as yourself'" (Matt. 22:37–39). Through both the Old and New Testaments, God's purpose for us remains unchanged: *love.*

But Paul understands that this world will shout other messages, and so we must renew our minds in order to discern the path God is asking us to walk.

I can't recognize opportunities to love my husband—my literal neighbor doing life shoulder to shoulder—if I don't renew my mind.

The Greek word translated as "renew" is *anakainōsei,* which means a renewal or change of heart or life, or as *Thayer's Greek Lexicon* explains, "a renovation, complete change for the better."[1] Isn't that what we all want and need?

If you had a fight with your husband or unraveled on your roommate . . . If you purposefully cut off someone in traffic or gossiped behind a friend's back . . . If you carry the weight of past mistakes too ugly to name . . . God sees you in your sin and has already proven His unconditional love for you. Right where you are. Respond to His love by renewing your mind in His Word today and every day.

Receive His love and kindness . . . and get ready to give it away.

What does renewing your mind look like for you? For example: listening to worship music, listing God's promises, or journaling your prayers. Choose one verse from today's study, write it down on a sticky note or index card, and read it every day.

Think of a current relationship or situation. How might God be asking you to demonstrate the same unconditional love you have received from Him? What could it look like to show up with courageous kindness today?

Reflect on this prayer and make it your own today:

Father, thank You for loving me right where I am no matter what I've done. Thank You for filling in the gaps of my poor choices, defensiveness, and sarcasm with Your grace. Help me to understand the depth of Your love for me. Empower me to show that same love and kindness to the neighbors inside and outside my own walls today. Amen.

Then the LORD passed by in front of him and proclaimed, "The LORD, the LORD God, compassionate and gracious, slow to anger, and abounding in lovingkindness and truth."

Exodus 34:6 NASB

My friend Tat Blackburn was killed in a car accident when she was twenty years old. It's easy to talk well about people after they've died, as if their faults died with them, but Tat was truly as good as everyone said she was. She loved Jesus in a rare way—He was her personal Friend, and she seemed to wake every day and walk alongside Him. Her love for Jesus was tender; it reminded me of a delicate flower you hold gently in your hands.

It felt like the world came to a stop the day Tat died. I was certain the wind ceased and the sun stood still. I had just gotten home from completing a summer internship in England. Between the shock, the stabbing grief, and the jetlag, I had never been so tired.

I talked to Tat's dad on the phone, and we both wept. Eventually, I crawled into bed. I didn't even know how to pray.

That night, God gave me a dream. I saw Tat. She was with Jesus.

She was wearing a gauzy white dress, and her hair was long and flowing even though she'd recently cut it. Her hand was entwined with Jesus's hand, and her facial expression was filled with a kind of adoration I had never seen here on earth.

Jesus was gazing down at her, delight pouring like sunshine from all of His facial features. I could feel the warmth radiating from Him, even though I knew I was not there. Tat's smile extended, and she tilted her head back. And then she laughed.

I woke up. Tears streamed down my face. I could still see the dream in my mind: Tat and Jesus, hand in hand.

As I've thought about that dream over the years, I can now name what I couldn't when the pain was so great. That dream was the kindness of God. It is a stunning picture of His heart—that on the night of my friend's death, He'd let me see where she is now in a dream. Even though Tat is gone from earth, she is very much alive in the presence of Jesus.

I cry just thinking of it. I'll hold on to that truth, that promise, and that example of God's kindness forever.

—ALIZA LATTA

How have you experienced God's kindness in an unexpected way at a time when you most needed it?

_____

_____

_____

_____

Yesterday we saw how God proved His love for us in the most radical act of kindness and sacrifice: by sending His Son to die for our sins. Today we're going to look at why. Why would God do that? What would compel the Creator of the universe to love people—liars and cheaters and disobeyers—and give up that which was most valuable and precious to Him?

To answer this question—and it's crucial that we do—we must travel back much farther than when Jesus took on human flesh and was born in Bethlehem. We must go back to when God told Moses who He is.

This part of the story unfolded early one morning when Moses climbed Mount Sinai. This was not Moses's first mountaintop encounter with God. The Lord had spoken with His chosen leader many times before, "just as a man speaks with his friend" (Exod. 33:11). But this mountain meeting was the fulfillment of Moses's request to see God's glory and God's promise to proclaim His name before him. Imagine what it would have been like to see and hear what came next.

> Then the LORD came down in a cloud and stood there with him; and he called out his own name, Yahweh. The LORD passed in front of Moses, calling out,
>
> "Yahweh! The LORD!
>   The God of compassion and mercy!
> I am slow to anger
>   and filled with unfailing love and faithfulness.
> I lavish unfailing love to a thousand generations.
>   I forgive iniquity, rebellion, and sin." (Exod. 34:5-7 NLT)

Whoa! In the presence of one man, God made Himself known to humankind.

What words stood out to you as you read God's description of Himself? Write them down along with a brief explanation of what you think they mean.

Which of those words connects most deeply to your personal experience of who God is? Which one is hardest for you to believe or see in Him and why?

_____

_____

_____

_____

In an act of intimacy, God tells us His name: *Yahweh.* Most Bible translations represent this word as LORD. But when God reveals His name is Yahweh, it's not like saying, "Oh, my formal name is Rebecca, but you can call me Becky." Yahweh is not a title like Mom or Auntie or Madam President. Yahweh is God's *name*—and the significance of that can be hard for us to grasp.

In Western culture, a person's name might be chosen because of a specific meaning, or it might be a trendy word hyped by the latest celebrity, or it could be selected because it starts with the same letter as a group of older siblings. Not so in Hebrew culture. In his book *God Has a Name*, John Mark Comer explains that in the ancient Near Eastern culture of the Bible, "your name was your identity, your destiny, the truth hidden in the marrow of your bones. It was the one-word moniker for the truest thing about you—your inner essence." He says that in Scripture, "names are revelatory of the *nature* of a person."[2]

In other words, God isn't just saying, "Call me Yahweh." He's saying, "Understand who I am. See my character. Get to know me."

We have so much to unpack and understand from this groundbreaking, foundation-making passage in Exodus 34. Let's read it again from the New American Standard Bible and look at the first three key components, which may have stood out to you too: "The LORD, the LORD God, compassionate and gracious, slow to anger, and abounding in lovingkindness and truth."

Right away we learn that Yahweh is compassionate—full of compassion and merciful. And that He is gracious—showing unmerited favor. Being compassionate and merciful are inextricable from His character. It makes sense then that Yahweh is slow to anger. If God's very nature is empathetic and forgiving, then He's not some hot-tempered dad you have to walk on eggshells around. *No!* Yahweh is a patient Father with a robust threshold for the absurd and unintentional and outright disobedient actions of His often wayward children.

Read what happened in Exodus 32:1–14 before God proclaimed His name. What do you learn about God's character from the way He responds to Moses's plea? How does this foreshadow or reinforce what God says about Himself in Exodus 34:5–7?

In Exodus 33:12–23 we find another remarkable conversation between God and Moses. What is Moses worried about, and what request does he make? What kind of *courage* and *relationship* do you think it required for Moses to speak to God this way?

What an extraordinary God! Really, think about it. After the Israelites blew it big time by making their own idol of gold to worship, Moses pleaded his case while God *listened*. Then, God *relented*—He changed His mind. He showed mercy. Later, when Moses was feeling insecure about leading this unpredictable group of people into an unknown land, God promised, "My presence will go with you, and I will give you rest" (Exod. 33:14). Not only that, but when Moses needed *additional* assurance, God gave it above and beyond what was asked. "I will cause all my goodness to pass in front of you, *and* I will proclaim the name 'the LORD' before you" (v. 19).

How often have you received messages such as "You're too much," or "You blew it one too many times," or "Get it together and stop being so needy"? Maybe you heard this from a parent or spouse; maybe you felt it from a boss or coworker, a teacher or friend. Sometimes the messages we internalize become woven into our unconscious beliefs about God. But the Exodus narrative demonstrates that this is *not* how God thinks or feels or acts toward His people!

Don't you see it, friend? Who God says He is in Exodus 34 is exactly who He had already proved Himself to be in the previous chapters. *Abounding in love and faithfulness.* Yes, *this* is the kindness of God in action. He not only *feels* compassion for His people but also *acts* in love and faithfulness—or, as the NASB renders it, lovingkindness and truth.

Kindness is baked into God's name. It's who He is.

Kindness is baked into God's name. It's who He is. And who He is reaches into our everyday lives, in the middle of both the mundane and crisis days. His reminders are continual, creative, and personal. For Aliza, God's kindness came to her in a dream while she slept. For Moses, God's kindness came in a cloud on a mountaintop. His kindness is coming for you too.

What impresses your heart most about Yahweh's character and how He relates to His people in the passages we've studied today?

_____

_____

_____

_____

In what area of your life do you need to have an honest (and courageous) conversation with God? Write out your most desperate need, sorrow, or predicament here. Then wait expectantly for His kindness.

_____

_____

_____

_____

Reflect on this prayer and make it your own today:

Yahweh, thank You for being compassionate and gracious, slow to anger, abounding in love and faithfulness. Thank You for making Yourself known. No matter where I am or what I'm going through, Your kindness is reliable, steadfast, and true. Help me see You clearly in the words You've already written and in the story You are still writing in my life. Amen.

Be merciful, just as your Father also is merciful.

Luke 6:36

I heard feet plodding down the stairs—the same feet that had stomped up them only minutes earlier. The clock and my drooping eyes told me it was past everyone's bedtime, but here we were, all awake anyway. My daughter walked to my chair and sank to the floor, laying her head on my lap. "I'm sorry," she whimpered. "I didn't mean it."

Summoning all the patience in the universe, I calmly said, "It's okay to be upset. It's not okay to treat your family this way."

"I know!" she cried. "I don't want to act like that! I'm trying to be better!"

In the blink of a weary eye, my heart thawed. Was I still tired of fighting this child in the same way over the same things every day of our lives? Was I still frustrated at the lack of peace—not to mention respect and plain old obedience—in our family? Was it still wrong for my daughter to scream hateful words at her sister, her dad, and me? Yes, yes, and yes. Obviously.

But did I understand how it feels to want so badly to be good and yet be so completely incapable of actually doing it? Have I ever fallen to my knees in regret and shame and, yes, repentance? Do I trust my heavenly Father to offer me mercy upon mercy in His eternal kindness and love? Yes, yes, and yes.

Part of my job as a parent is to teach my children to obey. Helping them understand consequences—for good choices and bad ones—is my responsibility. But even more important than that, I'm commanded to love them as my Father loves me.

Sometimes that looks like late-night hugs and forgiveness for hateful words. Sometimes it looks like brushing and braiding hair, or helping clean a messy bedroom, or taking a forgotten homework assignment to school. These are things my daughter is supposed to be responsible for, things I said I would not do. But they are also acts of kindness I can offer when they're needed most—even if they haven't been earned. Just like my Father does for me.

—MARY CARVER

Have you ever had a hard time helping someone when it seemed undeserved? Share about that here.

_____

_____

_____

_____

Undeserved kindness is the undercurrent of God's great story of redeeming His people. On every page of Scripture, at every turn in human history, God does what He does for the sake of love, not because He has to. From creation to the cross, from the Red Sea to the resurrection, God demonstrates His unfailing love and kindness. Because, as we discussed yesterday, compassion, mercy, grace, and faithfulness are consistent with His character.

But second chances, love, and forgiveness can be harder for us, right? We're prone to impatience, irritation, bitterness, and tallying up wrongdoings. We are quick to size up the child, the spouse, the co-worker, or the neighbor who has a bad attitude or has dropped the ball or didn't respond nicely, and it makes us want to withhold whatever good we could give.

It's so much easier to be kind when someone is kind to us, to love those whom we deem lovable. Unfortunately, God doesn't call us to a life that's easy. But He does invite us to a life that is *full*—which starts with showing others the same undeserved kindness we've received.

> **Jesus doesn't mess around when it comes to telling us how we're supposed to treat people—all people, all the time.**

Jesus doesn't mess around when it comes to telling us how we're supposed to treat people—all people, all the time. Once when a large crowd was gathered around Him, Jesus said, "But I say to you who listen: Love your enemies, do what is good to those who hate you, bless those who curse you, pray for those who mistreat you" (Luke 6:27–28).

Read Jesus's entire message in Luke 6:27–36. Jot down some of the specific instructions Jesus gives. What do you think is the driving theme or lesson in these instructions?

What is Jesus asking us to do that He has already done Himself? What is the significance of verse 36?

"Be merciful, just as your Father also is merciful." In other words, be like Yahweh!

Do you hear the beautiful reverberations of what the Lord said to Moses on Mount Sinai in what Jesus says to the crowd when He comes down from a mountain after a night spent in prayer to the Father? Jesus's call for us to do good to those who hate us, bless those who curse us, and pray for those who mistreat us sounds a whole lot like *relenting* from treating people as they deserve and instead heaping on undeserved kindness. The only way we can possibly live out such a tall order is to allow God to work in our hearts so we can become more like Him—you know, "compassionate and gracious, slow to anger, and abounding in lovingkindness and truth" (Exod. 34:6 NASB).

But how do we become women who turn the other cheek, give our coat, hug the kid who spewed the hateful words, love without holding back, and keep lavishing undeserved kindness even when we don't feel like it? Growing in the character of God begins with listening.

What holds you back from really listening to and living out Jesus's command to do good to others?

Read Colossians 3:12–15 and then think of a challenging person or situation in your life. What would it look like for you to put on a posture of love and kindness toward them?

Do you ever feel like you're the exception to one of Jesus's rules? Like, if God *really* knew your situation—your awful boss or intolerable in-laws or meddling neighbors or how that woman at church always gives you the judgmental side-eye—then He wouldn't *actually* expect you to be kind to them. (It's okay, this is a safe place to admit it.)

It's human nature to protect ourselves from being taken advantage of, to desire truth and justice (or at least our own ideas of them) to prevail. But if God who *is* the rightful judge chooses to show mercy through Christ's death and resurrection, then how can we not also choose to show mercy to others in small and gritty everyday ways?

How much importance does Jesus place on the way we treat others? Consider this: today's passage from Luke 6 is part of Jesus's first sermon right after He chose the twelve disciples and made them apostles. It follows what are known as the Beatitudes—Jesus's breakdown of His countercultural, upside-down kingdom, where those who are poor and hungry are blessed and the rich and self-satisfied are warned. These teachings are foundational to Jesus's ministry! In the presence of a great multitude, He tells His disciples that loving people is *essential* to following Him.

We'll dive deeper into this later in our study, but it's worth noting here that in Jesus's *last* conversation with His disciples, He tells them, "Love one another. Just as I have loved you, you are also to love one another. By this everyone will know that you are my disciples, if you love one another" (John 13:34–35).

Those are clear, bold bookend instructions to Jesus's ministry—but they're not always easy to obey. No doubt they will require courage for us to carry out.

Have you ever received kindness from someone when you clearly didn't deserve it? How did it make you feel? What did you learn about God's mercy through that person's kindness?

Read James 1:22–25 and then reflect back over what you've heard from the Lord in today's lesson. How is God asking you to be a courageous doer of the Word?

Reflect on this prayer and make it your own today:

Father, thank You for all the big and small ways You've shown me mercy. I don't deserve any of it, yet You choose to lavish Your kindness on me. Please give me eyes to see and a heart willing to respond to opportunities to love others courageously, kindly, and counterculturally, right where I am. Amen.

Don't you see how wonderfully kind, tolerant, and patient God is with you? Does this mean nothing to you? Can't you see that his kindness is intended to turn you from your sin?

Romans 2:4 NLT

Have you ever prayed for something for a really long time and needed an answer from the Lord? I have. I prayed for seven years for a child of our own. I asked God to make a way.

One day the Holy Spirit led me to James 5:14, which says to go to the elders for prayer.

I told God, "That's embarrassing. What if I cry in front of a room full of people I don't know? I've told my story to others who haven't been respectful of my feelings. What if it happens again? I'm not sure my heart could handle it."

I shelved the idea. I was uncomfortable with what it would require. I disobeyed. I rejected God's leading based on my emotions and expectations.

A few months later, I finally called the church office and asked to be put on the agenda for the monthly elder prayer meeting. The assistant told me they were on a break for the summer and I'd have to wait.

What! Here I am finally being obedient and I have to wait? At first I was exasperated. But moments after I hung up the phone, I realized how patiently God had waited on me to obey—evidence of His very nature of love and kindness.

I used those months of waiting for the prayer meeting to repent. I asked God to forgive me for not listening to His answer to my prayers. I asked Him again to make me open to *His* ways.

The day for the prayer meeting finally came, and my husband and I sat in front of our church elders and told our story. I cried a little, but I wasn't embarrassed because I was being obedient. They circled around us and anointed our heads with oil. They spoke to God on our behalf. It was a beautiful, holy moment I'm thankful to have experienced.

I didn't feel any different afterward, but I had learned not to judge my situation based on my feelings. I was expectant that God would be glorified through the rallying of our faith. I just didn't realize how expectant I already was.

Two weeks later, I was extremely fatigued and not myself. To my surprise, I was pregnant. The doctor told me I had been pregnant for a month. If you're quick with math, you'll realize I was already pregnant with our daughter while the elders were praying over us.

I was once again overwhelmed by God's kindness. He had revealed my sin of disobedience and had given me space to repent and wait on His timing. Then God gave me the opportunity to still be obedient and be a part of His miracles, which reveals how forgiving and loving He is.

God's kindness is expressed in His call for us to obey. And He will always deliver something beautiful out of our repentance.

—STEPHANIE BRYANT

When have you delayed (or flat-out refused) being obedient to God? What happened?

By now the idea that we are flawed people who are loved by God is not a new concept. In addition to the many ways we've examined this truth over the previous three days, you can probably think of other examples in the Bible that support it. One of the most famous and oft-quoted verses in Scripture says it clearly for us again: "For God loved the world in this way: He gave his one and only Son, *so that* everyone who believes in him will not perish but have eternal life" (John 3:16).

Any time we see the words "so that," our ears should perk up! It's a transitional phrase that links cause and effect. God's love for the world caused Him to send Jesus as a sacrificial bridge *so that* we could cross over into right relationship with God both now and for eternity.

Do you see how amazing and miraculous this is? This invitation to live in the *so that*?

Like all miracles, it's about God and what He did or is doing or will yet do. In Stephanie's story, God was the one who acted and answered her prayers and put a child in her womb. Yet God often requires our obedience and belief before we see the fullness of His plan come to fruition. The key word for us today in John 3:16 is *believes*. Everyone who believes will get to live in the *so that* of God's love. The word translated as "believes" is the Greek word *pisteuó*, which means "believe something to be true and, hence, worthy of being trusted."[3] It comes from a root word that denotes placing one's faith in a person or thing, and it implies we are to entrust and commit our spiritual well-being to Christ.[4]

So at the foundation of our lives is God's love freely given to us. We just have to believe.

Read Matthew 8:5–13 and John 11:38–44. How is believing linked to seeing or experiencing God's power in your life?

How is believing important beyond our initial profession of faith? What kind of courage must it have taken for the centurion (Matt. 8) and Martha (John 11) to believe?

The kindness of God is interwoven all through the two miracle stories we just read. To heal a servant, to bring a brother back from the dead, to respond to the desires of people. Incredible! God intervened because He was compelled by love *so that* people could see His goodness and believe. Listen again to the words of Jesus while Lazarus was still lying dead in the tomb: "Didn't I tell you that if you believed you would see the glory of God?" (John 11:40).

Perhaps you're wondering, *So what does this have to do with our opening verse and Stephanie's story about repentance?* Throughout the Bible, we find story after story of good people who wanted to follow God but struggled with actually trusting God's plan. Think of Abram and how God promised to give him more descendants than stars in the sky. Yet when his wife remained barren into old age, Abram tried to make his own way by having a child with his wife's servant, which was *not* God's plan. Or think of Peter—*oh, impulsive, impetuous, passionate Peter!*—who both rebuked and denied Jesus.

And yet . . . when Abram and Peter and Stephanie repented and turned back to God in obedience and belief, they saw His glory.

As Paul writes, "Don't you see how wonderfully kind, tolerant, and patient God is with you? Does this mean nothing to you? Can't you see that his kindness is intended to turn you from your sin?" (Rom. 2:4 NLT).

Whether you're putting your trust in Jesus for the very first time or you've been walking with the Lord for decades, we all have sin in our lives. God's continual, inexhaustible love, patience, and kindness are how He woos us to repentance. Once we admit the ways we've tried to live by our own strength and follow our own path, *then* we can get back to loving God and loving others in the way He calls us to.

How has God's kindness led you to repentance? Is there anything you need to repent of today?

Read Luke 15:1–7. What does the parable say causes joy in heaven? What does this show about God's character and how He relates to people?

From the way God's kindness turns us from our sin, to the way He rejoices when we repent, to how He responds to our desires, God wants us to see His *glory*. Does that mean He will always heal our loved ones? Always place a baby in empty wombs? Always answer our prayers the way we want Him to? No. God is not a vending machine, so we have no guarantee that putting in our quarters of belief, obedience, and repentance will produce the result we want.

But we can still *pisteuó*. We can still believe God, entrust our well-being to Him, and commit to sharing His kindness with others.

Now, at some point throughout this study you might be tempted to think, *I don't have what it takes to live with courageous kindness.* Maybe kindness and compassion feel like personality traits you just don't have. Maybe you feel disqualified from being gentle or generous because of your own hard circumstances. Mark this page, and then if (or when) one of those thoughts creeps in, come back and read this:

God does not require your perfection; He invites your partnership.

God does not require your perfection; He invites your partnership. You don't have to be perfectly kind or perfectly courageous.

All we have to do is say yes to *believing*—to putting our trust in God. To say with both our lips and our lives, "Lord, I trust you. I trust your answers to the prayers I'm still praying. I trust that you will make a way when you ask me to obey. I trust that in all things you work for the good of those who love you. God, I'm willing to be an active partner in the good you have for me and for others."

This is the foundation of making a simple difference and growing in courageous kindness. Are you in?

Read Romans 8:28. The Greek word translated as "good" in this verse is *agathós*, which means "inherently (intrinsically) good; as to the believer, it describes what originates from God and is empowered by Him in their life, through faith."[5] How does this definition of the good God works on our behalf deepen your understanding of His kindness?

Read Romans 2:4 again, along with Psalm 139:23–24. How will you let God's kindness lead you to live courageously for Him this week?

Reflect on this prayer and make it your own today:

Lord, thank You for loving me so much and for giving Your Son so I can have eternal life with You. Help me choose to trust and obey Your ways today. When I'm tempted to rely on my own feelings or fears more than Your Word, remind me of Your kindness and that You are working all things for my good. I believe in You, Jesus, and I'm ready to see Your glory! Amen.

Everyone should look not to his own interests, but
rather to the interests of others.

Philippians 2:4

I have spent a good twenty years serving in youth ministry in some capacity. I have had the tremendous honor
of mothering a number of junior high and high school girls,
sometimes stepping in as a bonus mom or even the only
mother some of them had ever known. All of those sweet
girls are in their mid to late twenties now, and it brings me
great joy to still be in relationship with many of them.

One young woman in particular has allowed me to walk with her
through extreme highs and lows over the past decade. Married with a
beautiful baby and another one on the way, she has come such a long
way, but she is still learning to navigate life and relationships.

Recently we were visiting at her house, just hanging out, and she
mentioned how badly she wanted to be productive while she had some
energy. So after I fed the baby dinner and she put her to bed, we got
to work folding laundry, washing dishes, and picking up all the baby
toys. She never asked for my help, but I knew how much she needed it,
so I didn't hesitate. It was never a question of whether or not I wanted
to help or if I would be willing to help. Of course I wanted to, and of
course I was willing! I love her and want God's best for her and her
family.

Such opportunities to jump in and serve a friend remind me of what God did for us. God didn't wait for us to ask for help before sending Jesus. He saw us in our need, our lack, our insufficiency, and He chose to do what only He could. During His time on earth, Jesus tangibly loved everyone He encountered. He made them feel seen and known. He fed them. He healed them. And He often did so without being asked. He put His love into action right where He was. May we take our cues from Him and do the same.

—KARINA ALLEN

When has someone jumped in and helped you without being asked? How did their actions communicate their love for you?

This week we've soaked in the truth of who God is—*Yahweh*, our compassionate and gracious God, slow to anger, abounding in loving-kindness and truth. We've remembered how God doesn't need us to fix ourselves or get things right on the first try in order to earn His favor. He loves us even in our sin and pursues us with kindness.

Now it's time to take what we've learned about God loving us right where we are and start grappling with what it means to love others in the same way. In other words, what does it look like for us to embrace a life of courageous kindness and mark the world with love in Jesus's name?

If you've read *The Simple Difference*, you're familiar with a prayer that says, "Lord, as I go on my way, have your way with me." In the same way that God loves you right where you are, He also calls you to love others exactly where they are. Courageous kindness isn't so much about going out of our way to be loving and kind, but intentionally living with eyes wide open to opportunities and hearts surrendered in obedience to demonstrate the love and kindness of Christ in our ordinary, everyday lives.

As we saw in the opening story, Karina was simply hanging out at her friend's house. While she was there, she saw the opportunity to love, serve, and show kindness to the person right in front of her. Karina could have let the moment pass by—but instead she embraced it.

Jesus modeled this same on-your-way, right-where-you-are mentality throughout His ministry.

Read Matthew 8:14–15; Luke 17:11–19; and John 2:1–11. Where was Jesus and what did He do in each of these passages?

_____

_____

_____

_____

What do the variety of settings and circumstances tell you about how Jesus saw opportunities to love people?

_____

_____

_____

_____

Whether He was at a wedding, in a friend's home, or on the road traveling, Jesus loved the people in front of Him. Now, granted, we probably won't be going around turning jugs of water into wine or healing leprosy, but we *can* follow Jesus's lead and be willing to meet the needs of others right where we are, often in unexpected ways.

In John 2, when Jesus's mom brings the wine shortage to His attention, Jesus isn't shy in pointing out that His ministry has not yet started. "'What does that have to do with you and me, woman?' Jesus asked. 'My hour has not yet come'" (John 2:4). His question shows an honest reaction—*this is not my responsibility*. His follow-up statement speaks to the fact that Jesus isn't ready for people to know who He really is.

One of the exciting things about this story is how it echoes what we saw with God and Moses back in Exodus. God listens to people and shows compassion. While Jesus may have preferred to stay under the radar at the wedding, He chose to honor His mom's request, meet the need in front of Him, and show kindness to everyone at the wedding.

He put the needs and desires of others above His own, which is exactly the posture of kindness that Paul writes about in Philippians. "Do nothing out of selfish ambition or conceit, but in humility consider others as more important than yourselves. Everyone should look not to his own interests, but rather to the interests of others" (Phil. 2:3–4).

Think of a time when you were aware of a need and thought, *That's not really my responsibility*, or, *I'd rather not get involved*. How might you see that situation differently in view of Paul's words and Jesus's examples?

Read Philippians 2:3–11. Write in your own words what it means to "adopt the same attitude" (CSB) or "have the same mindset" (NIV) as Christ.

_____

_____

_____

_____

Just like Jesus, we can love and serve others in our daily lives. The question is whether we'll be ready and willing to lay down our own interests for the sake of another. When Karina saw the pile of laundry and her friend's hungry baby, she could have tapped out and politely left in favor of going home to rest or do her own chores. When Jesus went into Peter's house back in Matthew 8, He was likely seeking rest and refreshment. But when He saw that Peter's mother-in-law was sick with a fever, He chose to attend to her needs first.

These are the daily choices we will get to make when pursuing a life of courageous kindness. We can live with a mentality that says, "I'll go out of my way to be kind when I have extra time or enough money." Or we say, "As I go on my way, Lord, have Your way with me."

> **"As I go on my way, Lord, have Your way with me."**

Paul's encouragement to the believers in Galatia is timely for us today. "So let's not get tired of doing what is good. At just the right time we will reap a harvest of blessing if we don't give up. Therefore, whenever we have the opportunity, we should do good to everyone—especially to those in the family of faith" (Gal. 6:9–10 NLT).

Whenever we have the opportunity—at a wedding, at a friend's house, or on our way somewhere—let's be women who are ready to show the kindness of Christ.

List opportunities that you have to do good to others in your daily and weekly on-your-way life.

_____

_____

_____

_____

Read Galatians 5:22–25. Note how this precedes Paul's exhortation in chapter 6 to do good to everyone. What does it mean to keep in step with the Spirit? How will that help you grow the fruit of the Spirit in your life?

_____

_____

_____

_____

Reflect on this prayer and make it your own today:

Jesus, thank You for showing us what it looks like to live with courageous kindness. Teach me how to walk in step with Your Spirit. Train my eyes to see opportunities to do good right where I am today and as I go on my way. Thanks for loving me just as I am. Help me to love others like that too. Amen.

▶ For a deeper look at this week's study and to spur on discussion if you're working with a small group, watch a FREE video from (in)courage at incourage.me/biblestudy.

exactly what you have

For we are God's masterpiece. He has created us anew in Christ Jesus, so we can do the good things he planned for us long ago.

Ephesians 2:10 NLT

I'm a lifelong Southerner, Georgia-born of sanguine clay. I adore our peculiarities—droppin' *g*'s from the end of words, frying just about everything, and understanding the art of biscuit making. But I cherish our sacred traditions—handwritten thank-yous, family reunions, chasing lightning bugs on hot summer nights.

Bless her heart . . .

Fixin' to cook dinner . . .

Cuttin' on a light . . .

Indeed, we have our particular words and ways. Like *surcie*, an old Southern term with no definitive spelling, which was introduced to me by my college roommate when I was battling a nasty cold.

"I got you a *surcie*!" Cassie boomed, plopping a box of name-brand tissues on my desk. Puzzled, I asked, "*What* did you just say . . . ?" Cassie repeated herself, adding a definition: a thoughtful little love gift, invaluable for reasons more important than money.

As I blew my nose for the eleven hundredth time, I understood. Cassie and I were college-broke, and soft tissues were an extravagance. But I was obviously miserable—my poor nose resembled a mealy tomato thanks to sandpaper disguised as dorm TP—and she knew the small gift would make a big difference.

Surcies reflect an intimacy in friendship and carry equal joy in giving and receiving. Because they're accompanied by the thoughtful intention of the giver, the best ones are remembered the rest of your life. How else can you explain remembering a box of Kleenex thirty-five years later?

If we're listening to the world's view that bigger is better or value is commensurate with a price tag, it's tempting to think a small gift isn't enough. This is when it's helpful to consider counsel from God's Word. There we learn what God thinks of small offerings and all He can do with them.

It is in the context of human limitations that we're able to see God's supremacy and power. In John 6:1–13, a young boy offered his lunch to help feed a crowd; Jesus transformed it into a feast with leftovers. In Mark 12:41–44, a widow gave a pittance for an offering. Jesus looked into her heart and knew she had given from her scarcity, while many rich people proportionally gave little.

In the upside-down economy of God, smallness is what creates the space for us to be able to see His power and immensity. Size is irrelevant when we give wholeheartedly. Gifts rooted in thoughtfulness and offered in love can change the world.

—ROBIN DANCE

When has someone given you something small that made a big impact in your day or even your life?

Welcome to week 2 of *Courageous Kindness*. Last week was all about understanding the character of God and how His lovingkindness reaches us exactly where we are. This week we're shifting our focus to the ways God calls us to impact the world with love and kindness.

Sometimes the most courageous thing you can do is believe that God can use exactly what you have—no matter how seemingly small or insignificant—to make a difference. Changing the world in Jesus's name isn't based on having a certain number of Instagram followers or bank account dollars. Rather, we get to show up with what we've got, give it freely, and watch the power of God work through our simple acts of intentional kindness.

> **We get to show up with what we've got, give it freely, and watch the power of God work through our simple acts of intentional kindness.**

In his letter to the Ephesians, Paul explains how God's transforming love and kindness toward us is the foundation of our ability to go and do likewise. Eugene Peterson says it like this in The Message:

> Now God has us where he wants us, with all the time in this world and the next to shower grace and kindness upon us in Christ Jesus. Saving is all his idea, and all his work. All we do is trust him enough to let him do it. It's God's gift from start to finish! We don't play the major role. If we did, we'd probably go around bragging that we'd done the whole thing! No, we neither make nor save ourselves. God does both the making and saving. He creates each of us by Christ Jesus to join him in the work he does, the good work he has gotten ready for us to do, work we had better be doing. (Eph. 2:7-10)

Apart from God, we can try to be moral people and do nice things for others; so-called random acts of kindness have been praised both inside and outside the church. But Paul is pointing out that as believers, our salvation is what empowers us to make a difference and guide others to Jesus.

We aren't saved by our good works. Yet God invites us to partner with Him in showing love and kindness to all humanity.

Read the fuller passage in Ephesians 2:1–10. Write down your observations or what stands out most to you. How does this connect back to what you learned in week 1?

_____

_____

_____

_____

When have you witnessed or received someone's kindness or good deed and recognized it as a reflection of their relationship with Christ? What is the mark of someone who is partnering with Jesus?

_____

_____

_____

_____

In our opening story, we learn that Robin's roommate gave her a surcie—what Cassie explained as "a thoughtful little love gift." Indeed, it was Cassie's thoughtfulness that meant as much to Robin's heart as the box of luxurious tissues did to her nose. Thoughtfulness—giving thought to, for, or about someone else—really is the foundation of kindness. Before Cassie could give Robin a gift, she had to be aware of her friend's need.

Jesus's life on earth was marked by thoughtful awareness of others. In Luke 19 we find a stunning example of this with a tax collector named Zacchaeus. The story begins with Jesus entering Jericho, where a large crowd had gathered to see the famous miracle-working teacher. In his book *Moments with the Savior*, Ken Gire imagines the scene unfolding like this:

> People are draped over windowsills like laundry hung out to dry, watching. A thick fringe lines the rooftops and looks down. On the street are huddles of curiosity—holy men and housewives, shopkeepers, teachers, traders, businessmen, bakers—elbow to elbow.
>
> Suddenly Jesus stops. He looks up at Zacchaeus. Shafts of the Savior's love filter through the branches. A long-awaited dawn shines on a despised tax collector. And a warmth begins to stir the cold darkness of his soul.[1]

He looks up. Three life-changing words.

Read the full story in Luke 19:1–10. Think about the crowd and all the possible sights, sounds, and smells that would have been vying for Jesus's attention as He entered a new city. What does it tell you about Jesus that He gave His attention to Zacchaeus?

_____

_____

_____

_____

Why do you think Zacchaeus was so quick to change his ways? (Think back to Romans 2:4 and Ephesians 2:4–5.) What impact do you think Jesus's kindness toward Zacchaeus might have had on the crowd?

_____

_____

What's remarkable about this moment is how the simple act of noticing and acknowledging someone made the biggest impact. Jesus, in His divine omniscience, knew full well the long list of Zacchaeus's sins. Jesus knew the depths of his deceptions, knew every time the chief tax collector had cheated or manipulated people to fill his own pockets. Jesus could have easily chosen to call the guy out. He could have publicly named his sins and shamed him in front of the crowds.

But what did Jesus do instead? He saw Zacchaeus just as he was and welcomed him. Instead of spending those moments under the sycamore tree rebuking Zacchaeus, Jesus wanted to spend time building a relationship. *Come down. I want to stay at your house.* Those may be words the rich man had never heard before.

Proverbs 16:24 says, "Kind words are like honey—sweet to the soul and healthy for the body" (NLT).

The good work God prepared in advance for you to do may be as simple as offering a box of Kleenex to a sick friend, taking a meal to a mom with a new baby, sharing a kind word with a stranger, or seeing someone on the fringes and saying, "Come on over here. I want to get to know you." What if it's just that simple?

Robin wrote, "Sometimes it's tempting to think a small gift isn't enough." How have you discounted the impact a small act of noticing, speaking, or giving could make? What truth from today's lesson will spur you on in the good work God has for you?

Look up Psalm 8:3–4. What does it mean that God is mindful of you? How has God looked after you and remembered you?

_____

_____

_____

_____

Reflect on this prayer and make it your own today:

God, thank You for noticing me. You loved me in my sin and invited me to a new life with You. I want Your love and kindness to overflow from me into others. Help me to use what I have, no matter how small, to make a lasting impact in someone's life today. Amen.

There's a young boy here with five barley loaves and
two fish. But what good is that with this huge crowd?

John 6:9 NLT

As we disembarked from the plane, I lugged an over-stuffed diaper bag, my backpack, and a carry-on suitcase with a wayward wheel. I tried to direct my daughters to walk carefully down the stairs while my husband, Ericlee, manned the rest of the carry-ons and car seats.

The Haiti humidity hit us in the face like a heavy blanket. We snaked our way through customs for what seemed like hours and finally made it to the curb to meet our friend, Pastor Peter. We climbed into his truck and began our long, bumpy journey to the mission house.

As we drove, Peter caught us up on all the things related to the non-profit we had helped start in the northern mountains. Then he turned to me and said, "I need your help. I want to start a jewelry business for the women in our churches."

Jewelry? My interest was piqued. Jewelry-making had been one of my hobbies since I was a little girl.

Peter explained that he was burdened for the people in his church who were living in the chains of poverty. He wanted to find sustainable income for them rather than handouts. He sent a few ladies from the church to learn how to make jewelry from a woman who lived in Port-au-Prince. He hoped they could teach others the craft and then sell the items locally and in the US.

For months, Ericlee and I had prayed that God would prepare us for whatever work He had for us in Haiti. It was hard for me as a planner to not know what I was stepping into.

But God knew.

I never dreamed He would take a hobby I had when I was younger and transform it into a ministry and business.

I still remember so vividly the day I first met the women. They made a circle with chairs in the shade of the church building. I was too timid to use my Haitian Creole, so I just watched them work.

One woman cut cardboard from cereal boxes into triangle-shaped strips. Other women took the cardboard strips and began rolling them around skewers to create beads. They glued the beads in place and dried them in the sun. While they worked, the ladies chattered and their kids played in the schoolyard nearby. This was not just a way for the women to make money but also a way for them to cultivate community.

I had no business experience, but I loved making jewelry, and my heart was to disciple women in God's Word. God took what little I had to offer and multiplied it. Through the years, our community grew to employ sixty artisans through the Haitian Bead Project. They continue to provide for their families through the creative work of their hands.

—DORINA LAZO GILMORE-YOUNG

Has God ever asked you to use something seemingly irrelevant—an old hobby, a forgotten talent, or a small treasure—to make a difference? What does Dorina's story tell you about God's ability to meet the needs of His people?

As we think about living with courageous kindness to be agents of change for God's kingdom, it's important that we understand this: we're responsible for giving what we have; God is responsible for the difference it makes.

We get to be obedient; God gets to handle the outcome.

Perhaps the most iconic example of this is the boy who gave his five loaves of bread and two fish. If you're not familiar with the story, it's found in all four of the Gospels (Matt. 14:13–21; Mark 6:30–44; Luke 9:10–17; John 6:1–15). That fact alone points to its significance in Scripture and in the ministry of Jesus. Here's a super quick recap.

> **We're responsible for giving what we have; God is responsible for the difference it makes.**

A huge crowd—five thousand men, plus women and children—was following Jesus and His disciples, eager to see Him heal the sick. They were in a remote location. It was getting late, which was a problem because there wasn't any food to feed the crowd, and there was no place to buy some. Plus, as Philip points out in the John 6 account, "It would take more than half a year's wages to buy enough bread for each one to have a bite!" (v. 7 NIV).

That's when Andrew, another disciple, piped up, "Here is a boy with five small barley loaves and two small fish, but how far will they go among so many?" (v. 9). In essence he's saying, "Look at what we have—it's something, but it's not enough."

Think of a time when you were aware of a huge problem and your resources to help fell painfully short. Did you give what you had anyway? What was the outcome?

Read John 6:1–13. How might you have felt if you were one of the disciples trying to solve this problem? What do you notice about Jesus's demeanor and actions?

"Have the people sit down," Jesus said. Imagine a softness to His tone—not like an exasperated dad trying to tame a toddler but like a friend inviting friends to rest and share a meal.

From the other Gospel accounts of this story, we know that it was getting late, they were in a deserted location, and the disciples were worried. Stressed. But Jesus didn't bark out a bunch of orders to the disciples or take a poll to see who was hungriest or ask for volunteers to go home. In a situation that could have been on the brink of chaos— five thousand potentially hangry men is no joke!—Jesus guided the crowd into a peaceful posture of receiving.

Then Jesus took what was available—five small loaves of bread and two fish—and He gave thanks. Before the crisis had been solved, Jesus showed expectant gratitude for what was given and what God could do.

Look up Psalm 5:3; Psalm 107:8–9; and 1 Thessalonians 5:16–18. Write down key words from each passage.

How can having a posture of expectant gratitude prepare us to courageously give what we have and to receive what God gives?

Now let's turn our attention to the boy who gave his little lunch. Scripture doesn't say whether he offered his meager meal willingly or begrudgingly. Did he hold out hope that it would help, or did it feel like an empty gesture toward a lost cause? We don't know. What we do know is that Jesus transformed what was not enough into more than enough.

And here's the thing we need to understand: what we think about our resources doesn't dictate or limit God's power to use them. It wasn't up to the boy what became of his food. It was up to him to be aware of the needs around him, assess his resources, and respond with generosity and kindness.

This amazing miracle of multiplication was fueled by God's power! Only He could take total lack and turn it into total satisfaction. But the spark that started the blaze of provision was one small act of obedience.

In our opening story, Dorina shared about her love for making jewelry and discipling women. But did that qualify her to help the poverty problem in Haiti? God didn't ask her to solve the whole problem; He just asked her to say yes to offering what she had so He could multiply it. Dorina's obedience helped change the lives of sixty artisans and their families.

To live with courageous kindness, we have to exchange the way we see our not-enough for the way God sees it. We don't have to carry the burden of solving a big problem or fixing a complex system on our own. God cares about the one, the sixty, the five thousand. He is eager to meet the needs of His children and invites us to be a part of that.

What problem is heavy on your heart today? Maybe it's something global like human trafficking or something personal like a friend in crisis. What "loaves and fish" might God be asking you to offer?

Where in your life do you need a miracle of multiplication? Think about the resources you already have—no matter how small—and write them down. Then courageously give thanks for what's been provided and wait expectantly for God to multiply it.

Reflect on this prayer and make it your own today:

Jesus, thank You for showing us what it looks like to have a posture of expectant gratitude. Like the boy who gave his little lunch for the good of those around him, help me see opportunities this week to give what I have, no matter how small, and trust You to multiply it. I'm ready to see Your glory! Amen.

Truly I tell you, this poor widow has put more into
the treasury than all the others. For they all gave out
of their surplus, but she out of her poverty has put in
everything she had—all she had to live on.

Mark 12:43-44

I stood in my kitchen riffling through a small accordion
file where we keep money for our monthly budget. It
was the end of the month, so the file was mostly empty.
My sister was coming over soon, and I was scrambling to
find some cash to give her. I checked my wallet. The jar
where we stash dollars to save for vacation. My bottom
desk drawer. All the places I might have hidden a few extra
bucks.

My search was semi-successful. I thumbed through the wad of cash.
Somehow I had found a hundred dollars. Strangely, though, they were
all five-dollar bills. Suddenly, twenty five-dollar bills felt like both too
much and painfully not enough. I wasn't sure what to do.

My sister was going through a hard time—a *really* hard time. Life
had imploded, and the gap between what she had and what she needed
seemed impossible to bridge. I wanted to support her, to let her know
that she wasn't alone. In some ways a hundred dollars felt embar-
rassingly inadequate, as I knew it would hardly make a dent in her
needs. On the other hand, I felt a little guilty that I had the resources to
scrounge up that sum of money and the sacrifice didn't hurt too much.

I stared at the stack of five-dollar bills. I didn't want to make my sister feel insulted or ashamed by my gift. I just wanted her to know that she was seen and that I would walk through the fire with her. "Lord, help me to know what to do," I prayed.

I felt a stirring in my spirit. The whisper of God that said, *I know your heart and will honor it. Give joyfully—exactly what you have.*

Later that afternoon, while cousins played together in the backyard and my sister and I cleaned up from lunch, I handed her a white envelope with my gift. She stuck it in her purse without opening it.

That night my phone binged with a new text: "Sister, I couldn't believe it when I opened your envelope. This morning at church I put my last five dollars in the offering plate. I knew God was asking me to trust Him, but it was hard. Your generous gift was God reminding me that He sees me and will be faithful to provide for me."

With tears in my eyes and a smile spread across my face, I stood once again in my kitchen, just shaking my head. Only God. His kindness to use and bless exactly what we have is abundant.

—BECKY KEIFE

Can you think of a time when God used something small or seemingly inadequate to meet your specific need or the need of someone else? Describe that here.

Too big or too small. Over-the-top or painfully not enough. No matter what we have to give, it's easy to fall into the trap of questioning if it can really make a difference.

I have an extra sandwich, but what if the homeless man doesn't want it?

I could hold the door for that woman in a wheelchair, but what if she would rather do it herself?

I could donate to that mission project or disaster relief, but what I have would barely make a dent in the gigantic need.

Do you ever find yourself sinking into this kind of thinking? We want to love God and others well, but it's easy to let doubt derail our obedience. To let what-if questions interfere with our desire to show kindness.

So in today's study we're going to unpack three important truths from Jesus's teaching:

> **We want to love God and others well, but it's easy to let doubt derail our obedience.**

1. Obeying God is an overflow of our love for Him.
2. The Holy Spirit will help us know how to obey and to love others.
3. God honors and accepts whatever we give in His name, no matter the size of the gift.

Read John 15:7–12. What is the connection between love and obedience? What three things does Jesus desire most from us? (Hint: look at verses 8, 9, and 12.)

_____

_____

_____

_____

Turn to the previous chapter and read John 14:12–26. What similarities do you see in this passage and the one above? Thinking in a courageous kindness mindset, what might you ask of God today?

In the opening story, I shared how I felt unsure about what to give my sister, so I prayed for help and God guided me in what to do next. It's the fulfilment of exactly what Jesus promised in John 14! Do you see the progression?

Ask in Jesus's name. → Love God and keep His commands. → The Holy Spirit will guide you.

Look at how the same pattern repeats in John 15:

- "If you remain in me and my words remain in you, *ask* whatever you want and it will be done for you" (v. 7).
- "This is my command: *Love* one another as I have loved you" (v. 12).
- "When the Counselor comes, the one I will send to you from the Father—the *Spirit* of truth who proceeds from the Father—he will testify about me" (v. 26).

As women (and as people in general), we're pretty good at making things complicated. But God? He makes things surprisingly simple. He basically says, *I love you, and I invite you to love me too. The best way you can do that is by loving other people. But I won't even ask you to do that alone. I'll give you an Advocate, a Counselor, the Holy*

Spirit to teach you and guide you and be with you every step of the way.

Read Jesus's words to the disciples on His last night with them in John 16:13–14, 33. How do Jesus's promises give you courage? How can this help you keep His command to love others?

As we wrap up today's study, there's one more story we ought to consider when thinking about how God guides us in our giving and honors exactly what we have. Read Mark 12:41–44. Why do you think Jesus wanted His disciples to take note of what the woman gave?

There's so much to consider in these four verses. First, was Jesus the only person keeping a watchful eye on the collection box? Perhaps seats near the offering box were prized. The fact that Jesus drew specific attention to the widow's gift might imply that other people had their attention fixed on the larger gifts. Maybe ears perked up when a deluge of coins poured into the collection box, the fast and furious clink of metal on metal a signal of the giver's religious piety and prestige. But when the steady stream of coins was replaced with two barely audible clinks, it wasn't worthy of anyone's attention—except Jesus's.

Second, have you ever wondered how the widow felt when giving her two small coins? Was she ashamed she didn't have more to offer the Lord? Was she afraid that giving all she had would leave her without food and shelter? In that moment she might have felt confident or humiliated, hopeful or defeated. The text doesn't say. But this we do know: Jesus esteemed her gift.

Regardless of how she felt about it or what onlookers in the temple thought about it, God called out the value of giving her all.

The world says, "Watch out for yourself; hoard what you have." But God says, "I am trustworthy. I will take care of you." God honors when we give our all, no matter how big or how small. He did it for two sisters and one poor widow. He will do it for you too.

Look up Luke 12:6–7, 22–34. What assurance of God's care does Jesus give? How have you experienced the kindness of God's provision in your life?

How can you courageously ask God to use you as an instrument of His kindness today? Write down one way that you can love others, and then trust Him to guide you and provide for you this week.

Reflect on this prayer and make it your own today:

*God, thank you for making living with courage and kindness
so simple: I just get to listen to Your voice, remain in Your love,
and follow where You lead. I'm so grateful You're not limited by
what I have; when I give my all, You honor it in ways I couldn't
imagine. Show me how to love someone in a tangible way
today. You are able; I'm available—and I trust You. Amen.*

Then the LORD said to Moses, "I am going to rain bread from heaven for you. The people are to go out each day and gather enough for that day."

Exodus 16:4

To this day, I can see my Bible study group crowded into my tiny living room. We were all in our twenties, figuring out how to be adults together and doing it with snacks and Scripture (in equal amounts, if I'm honest).

One night I couldn't focus on our discussion at all, distracted by financial struggles weighing heavy on my mind. Between circumstances and choices, my husband and I had found ourselves so deep in debt and so far behind on every bill that I could not see a way out. The problem was compounded by the intense shame I felt about all of it.

I didn't want to tell my friends what was keeping me awake at night. We had known each other for years and spent much of our free time together. We shared a lot, but not this. When it came time for prayer requests that night, though, I broke down. For the first time since I'd known these ladies, I told them what a mess our finances were. I told them how scared and angry and frustrated and embarrassed I was.

I wasn't sure how they'd react, what they'd say or do. But I certainly didn't expect what happened.

My friends huddled with me on the couch and on the floor around our coffee table, their eyes understanding and their arms comforting. They prayed for me—mighty prayers for supernatural solutions. And then they stayed, brainstorming with me ideas for ways to move forward. And not one person spoke a word of judgment or criticism. They left that night with more hugs and promises to keep praying.

Then, the next day, one of my sweet friends went a step further. When I returned home from work, I found an envelope in the mailbox with a Walmart gift card and a note that said she knew it wasn't much (it felt like so much!), but she hoped it would help us with groceries.

She didn't have to do that. Obviously, she didn't have to spend her own limited budget to help us. But she also didn't have to sign her name on that note. She could have sent it anonymously in an effort to protect my pride. Instead, she bravely included that note, because she wanted to make sure I knew—without a doubt—that she was with me and for me, that she loved me and wanted to help me.

That gift didn't make my money problems disappear. It didn't pay all my bills or pay off my credit card. But it did remind me that I wasn't alone, that I was loved, and that God would provide. And that is a kindness I'll never forget.

—MARY CARVER

Is it hard for you to be transparent and vulnerable with others about your needs or messy circumstances? What happens in friendships when we either withhold or divulge the hard of what's really happening in our lives?

How often do we feel alone in our mess? If you've ever looked at your life and wondered, *How did I get here?* you're not alone. Whether it's financial difficulties like Mary experienced in our opening story, failing relationships, a devastating diagnosis, or a life that just isn't playing out the way you had imagined, at some point the question comes, *Where is God in this?*

The Israelites found themselves in that same place. God had rescued them from slavery in Egypt through the unlikely leadership of Moses and the miraculous parting of the Red Sea. But after two months of wandering in the wilderness with no promised land in sight, the Israelites began asking those same questions: *How did we get here? Where is God in this?* In their hunger and confusion and desperation, the people complained and even longed to go back to their chains in Egypt so they could at least die with full bellies (Exod. 16:1–3).

If you're a parent, coach, or teacher, you know how easy it is to respond to griping children with harsh correction rather than gently addressing their need. Thankfully, God is a way better parent. His response? "I am going to rain bread from heaven for you. The people are to go out each day and gather enough for that day" (v. 4).

In other words, *I hear your cries. I see your plight. I will intervene in your circumstance and provide for your needs.*

Read the full account of God's miraculous manna provision in Exodus 16. When God asked people to collect only enough food for each day, what was He really asking them to do?

Some time after God first sent manna and quail from heaven, as the Israelites were camped out at the base of Mount Sinai, Moses met with God in that famous encounter where God proclaimed His name. (Think

back to week 1, day 2, and look up Exodus 34:5–7 as a refresher.) How was God's provision of manna a demonstration of His character?

God is mindful of His people—and He wants us to trust Him! If you've walked with the Lord for a long time, that's a reality that's easy to take for granted. If you're new to knowing and trusting God, the fact that He is aware of your needs and is willing to respond might not even be on your radar.

Earlier this week we looked at Psalm 8:4, where David asks, "What is mankind that you are mindful of them, human beings that you care for them?" (NIV). What a beautiful reminder of how vast God's power is and how intimately He's aware of His people.

God doesn't have to care for us. He doesn't have to offer His love or provision, compassion or forgiveness. So why does He choose to? *Because that is who He is.* People on the other hand? We're finicky and shifty and unstable. But God will not depart from His character.

Through the pages of Scripture and our own personal stories, we know that God's awareness of our needs doesn't equate to an easy and pain-free life. A gift card didn't wipe away Mary's debt, but it gave her enough hope in the moment to keep pressing forward. Often God's care and provision come in day-by-day, moment-by-moment doses.

How have you experienced the comfort of God's presence in a difficult circumstance? What physical, emotional, or spiritual needs will you ask Him to send manna-like provision for today?

Look up Psalm 26:2–3. How mindful are you of God's unfailing love? How has His kindness been evident in your life?

To the Israelites, God gave manna. To Mary, God gave a living room full of friends who loved her and a Walmart gift card. God is boundless in the ways He cares for His children—and the ways He invites us to partner with Him.

Do you or does someone you know need the reminder that God is mindful of our circumstances? As women of courageous kindness, we can join God in His work by caring for the people in our lives with whatever we have, right where we are.

> **We can join God in His work by caring for the people in our lives with whatever we have, right where we are.**

Mary's Bible study partners demonstrated courageous kindness in listening to the raw parts of her story and ministering to the tender parts of her heart by being there, accepting her, and praying for her. Sometimes we also have the opportunity to be God's manna-delivery girls—providing a fellow wanderer just what's needed for that day and reminding her that she is cared for.

Reflecting on today's lesson, how do you think it requires courage for us to both give and receive kindness?

Who in your life could use a reminder that they are loved and seen by God? What small kindness could you show today that might make a big impact for them?

Reflect on this prayer and make it your own today:

God, thank You for being mindful of me today. Thank You for seeing my needs, my mess, my predicament. Please send people and provision to remind me that I am not alone, and please help me to be that kind of friend to others. Give me a heart willing to respond in love and compassion to the needs in front of me. Make me a deliverer of manna, that others might see You and know You more. Amen.

And a woman in the town who was a sinner found out that Jesus was reclining at the table in the Pharisee's house. She brought an alabaster jar of perfume and stood behind him at his feet, weeping, and began to wash his feet with her tears. She wiped his feet with her hair, kissing them and anointing them with the perfume.

Luke 7:37-38

A few years ago, something tragic happened. It wasn't the first tragic thing I've experienced, but it was definitely something that changed my life in more ways than I can put into words. Steve, my friend of over a decade, passed away from cancer. He left behind his wife, Gayla, and their three kids all under the age of ten.

When his initial diagnosis came, everyone was rocked by it. Then helplessness set in.

I'm not a doctor or a grief counselor. What on earth could I possibly do to help? Anyone who knows me realizes that by nature I'm a doer. I'm a fixer and a problem solver. I feel most helpful when I'm serving others, especially those I love.

When Gayla first shared Steve's diagnosis with all our friends, everyone wanted to help, though we didn't fully know what that would look like. Gayla wasn't even sure what she needed. Eventually, though, she reached out to me and I babysat the kiddos. Everything after that became some of the sweetest and saddest moments I've ever walked through.

I've spent the last several years getting to be the hands and feet of Jesus to this precious family. It truly is more of a blessing to give than to receive. I became a regular part of their household, spending many days helping with kids, helping with Steve, doing laundry, hanging out for movie nights, and breaking bread together. More often than not, the midnight hour came and went. Those late nights hurt the next morning, but they gave me such life.

Long after most of our friends went back to life as usual, I had the privilege of sticking around through Steve's illness and after his passing. Day to day. Life on life.

My sweet friend recently moved out of state for a fresh start. I wept as Gayla broke the news and told me how God had ordained every step of this process. She shared how grateful she was for all of my sacrifice. I told her that it was in no way a sacrifice for me. It was actually my greatest joy.

—KARINA ALLEN

How would you describe the connection between sacrifice and kindness?

Sometimes sacrifice just feels like sacrifice—hard, painful, costly. And sometimes it is those things *and* it somehow becomes life-giving. Perhaps the difference lies in our focus. When our focus is on *what* we're giving up—like hours at the end of a long day, dollars in the middle of a stretched budget, or more patience when ours is shot—then giving becomes agonizing. But when we focus on *who* is receiving the benefit of our kindness, the ache of sacrifice is replaced with the joy of giving. And as Karina discovered, often our reward is not in reciprocity but in knowing our kindness made a difference in someone's life.

Today we're going to focus on two women in the Bible who demonstrate what it means to lavish kindness even when it's a sacrifice.

The first is a woman who is introduced with a label rather than a name: *sinner*. In Luke 7 Jesus was invited to eat at the home of a Pharisee named Simon. When a woman in town heard Jesus was there, she went to the house, where Jesus was reclining at the table. "She brought an alabaster jar of perfume and stood behind him at his feet, weeping, and began to wash his feet with her tears. She wiped his feet with her hair, kissing them and anointing them with the perfume" (vv. 37–38).

Read the full account in Luke 7:36–50. How did the Pharisee view the woman's actions? How was Jesus's outlook on her sacrifice different?

How do you think the woman felt in that moment as she poured perfume and tears and sacrifice on Jesus's feet? Have you ever felt so compelled to show love that you didn't care what other people thought?

In this story Jesus speaks volumes about faith and forgiveness. But for the sake of our study, let's zero back in on the woman. In addition to the fact that she is identified as a sinner, we learn that she is a woman who responds. She heard that Jesus was near. She recognized an opportunity to thank Him, love Him, and serve Him—and she took it.

Imagine the courage it required for her to show such humble, extravagant kindness—and how it must have felt to be ridiculed for it. To be vulnerable with her tears, her hair, her heart. Probably questioning if she was even worthy to touch the Savior's feet. Maybe wondering in the back of her mind if her lavish kindness that cost a year's wages was too big a sacrifice.

But she was willing to risk judgment, rejection, and hardship for the sake of kindness.

Think about how this plays out in your own life. You see an opportunity to worship God, show appreciation to a friend, or help a stranger. How do you respond? Do you worry that what you feel compelled to do is too much, too humbling, or too vulnerable?

> **It takes courage to listen to God's voice and give what we have, when and how and to whom He asks us to give it.**

It takes courage to listen to God's voice and give what we have, when and how and to whom He asks us to give it. Cleaning Jesus's dirty feet with her hair and tears and expensive perfume wasn't a small thing. It wasn't like buying a latte for the person behind you in line at Starbucks or giving your roommate a box of tissues. Small things like that *do* make a difference! But this was extravagant, over-the-top, sacrificial kindness—a perfect response to God's lavish love.

Look up Romans 12:10 and 1 Peter 4:10–11. Do the woman's actions in Luke 7 seem appropriate in light of these verses? Why or why not?

**What tends to hold you back from lavishing kindness on others (e.g.,
awkwardness, fear of judgment, worry about imposing or overstepping)?
How could Paul's instructions to "outdo one another in showing honor"
(ESV) give you courage?**

Let's move now to John 12, where a similar scene unfolds with
another woman and another jar of perfume. This time it's Mary, the
sister of Martha and Lazarus, who anoints Jesus's feet with expensive
perfume and wipes them with her hair. Her gift is also judged, but not
because she was deemed unworthy to give it, as the other woman had
been; Mary had a close friendship with Jesus, as we'll talk more about
in week 5. Rather, Judas Iscariot, the disciple who would later betray
Jesus, was indignant at Mary's extravagant act of service because the
perfume could have been sold for a high price and the funds given to
the poor (John 12:4–5).

How did Jesus respond? He told Judas, "Leave her alone; she has
kept it for the day of my burial. For you always have the poor with you,
but you do not always have me" (vv. 7–8).

Ouch. Well done, Jesus.

Our acts of kindness might be criticized—either because of who
we are or what we're giving—but Jesus welcomes us and our gifts! He
knows our hearts and He sees the whole picture.

While both Simon the Pharisee and Judas Iscariot questioned and
judged these women, Jesus's response affirmed them. He rebuked the
men for their impure motives and praised the women's kindness. This
was about far more than dirty feet and expensive perfume. It was about
repentance and forgiveness; their kindness was a foreshadowing of
God's love in the sacrifice Jesus would make. Though the women were

criticized, their actions were recorded for all humanity to learn from and remember.

Any way we can pour out our lives for others pales in comparison to the love-soaked blood that Jesus spilled for us.

Read Colossians 3:12–13. (We looked at these verses last week, but they bear repeating!) Based on John 12:3, which of these characteristics did Mary put on or "clothe" herself in?

_____

_____

_____

Is there something God is asking you to sacrifice as an act of worship and kindness? Write down any ideas or nudges from the Holy Spirit and ask God to give you courage to respond.

_____

_____

_____

Reflect on this prayer and make it your own today:

Jesus, thank You for being a fierce defender of women who worship You and a gracious receiver of the gifts we humbly give. I want to be a woman of courageous kindness who isn't afraid of what other people will say or think, but who is willing to love fully for Your sake. Help me to love courageously today. Amen.

> For a deeper look at this week's study and to spur on discussion if you're working with a small group, watch a FREE video from (in)courage at incourage.me/biblestudy.

bending low and lifting up

While he was preaching God's word to them, four
men arrived carrying a paralyzed man on a mat. They
couldn't bring him to Jesus because of the crowd, so
they dug a hole through the roof above his head. Then
they lowered the man on his mat, right down in front of
Jesus.

Mark 2:2–4 NLT

Though we're not extremely close, I have a great relationship with my sister-in-law (my brother's wife). Our kids are similar in age, and we text each other several times a week about them, as well as to share recipe recommendations. And when I think of the times in my life when someone has bent low to serve me, she comes to mind.

Each of us, for different reasons, has had difficult pregnancy experiences. During one of my pregnancies, I was so exhausted and sick that cooking and cleaning for my family felt completely overwhelming and daunting. In desperation, I texted my sister-in-law and asked if she would cook a meal or two for us. Looking back, it felt so embarrassing to have to ask outright for such a big help. But instead of making me feel even more pitiful than I already did, she just said yes.

She arrived at my house with a sack of ingredients that she turned into delicious meals. Next, she pulled out a bucket of cleaning supplies and literally bent down and scrubbed the toilets. And then she knelt again and painted my toenails. My feet were so swollen and puffy by that point in my pregnancy, it's hard to know which act of service I appreciated the most!

That day, my sister-in-law showed humility by pampering my feet and scrubbing our toilets. She showed compassion by saying yes to my big ask for meals. In all her time with me that day, she showed care and kindness. She put my needs above her own and just showed up ready to serve.

What a gift she gave me that day! Her act of kindness certainly blessed me through and through.

—ANNA E. RENDELL

Do you have a hard time asking for help? What holds you back from inviting someone into your needs?

It takes courage—and a healthy dose of humility—to ask someone for help when we're feeling desperate. We've all been there, right? Overwhelmed by regular life and then the whole family gets hit with the stomach flu. Or the storm comes and the basement floods. Or the job doesn't come through and the rug gets pulled out from under you. We can grin and bear it (or cry alone while drowning in our debt, disease, grief, or fatigue), or we can bravely admit we're not okay—we need help making it through another day.

Courage and humility are also needed when stepping into someone else's need. These two qualities are cornerstones for living the simple difference—a life marked by intentional kindness. Anna's opening story beautifully displays this reality on both sides.

We're going to kick off this week by looking at another story that does this. Found in three of the four Gospels, it's the story of a man who couldn't walk and a group of friends who carried him to Jesus.

Jesus had recently returned home to Capernaum, and people had come from Jerusalem and all over Galilee and Judea to hear Him teach. In Mark 2 the scene unfolds like this:

> Soon the house where he was staying was so packed with visitors that there was no more room, even outside the door. While he was preaching God's word to them, four men arrived carrying a paralyzed man on a mat. They couldn't bring him to Jesus because of the crowd, so they dug a hole through the roof above his head. Then they lowered the man on his mat, right down in front of Jesus. (vv. 2–4 NLT)

News of the teacher with the power to heal had spread far and wide. Everyone wanted a chance to be near Jesus and witness the power of His miraculous touch. But who wanted it most?

Have you ever considered whose idea it was to go see Jesus in the first place—the paralyzed man or his friends? Read the full account in Mark 2:1–12. Imagine the man asking his friends to take him to see Jesus. How do you think he felt when getting there turned into a big production and a dramatic entrance?

On the flip side, maybe it was the man's four friends who initiated carrying him to Jesus. What if they were the ones desperate and determined to help their friend secure his one chance to be healed? What does this story show about their character?

Scripture doesn't spell out the life story of the man on the mat or his relationship with the four men who brought him before Jesus. What is clear is that they chose to bend low for the sake of lifting up a brother.

Like with Anna's sister-in-law, these guys didn't give just the bare minimum. Anna asked for a couple of meals, but she also got clean toilets and pretty toes because her sister-in-law saw greater opportunities to serve her family. The paralyzed man probably asked simply to be taken to the house where Jesus was. When they arrived and found it bursting with people, the friends could have said, "We got you here like you asked, but it's so crowded there's no way we can all squeeze in. So sorry, man." They could have left it at that. But they didn't.

Instead, the four guys were determined to get their friend in front of Jesus. They found the outdoor staircase, which was common to ancient Middle Eastern homes, and made their way to the roof. Perhaps the man they carried was light and maneuvering him up the narrow stairs was easy. Or maybe he was heavy and each step caused their backs to strain, their arms to burn. Once on the roof, they knelt down and started digging through the hard-packed, sun-dried mud with their bare hands and dismantling the support branches laid across wood ceiling beams.[1] Dirt lodged beneath their fingernails as sweat beaded on their brows.

Their devotion to their friend and their faith in Jesus's power to heal him compelled them to keep going.

When daylight finally broke through to the room below, they had to muster even more courage and might. Two men likely jumped down first, startling the crowd with their audacity to interrupt Jesus's teaching. The two men on top bore the weight of their friend's ailment, lowering his body to the arms outstretched to receive him. Ready to bring him to Jesus.

Four guys chose to do for another what they surely would have wanted someone to do for them. It's the reverberation of God's heart song—calling us to love one another with the same fierce kindness He shows to us.

> **God's heart song is calling us to love one another with the same fierce kindness He shows to us.**

Read Matthew 7:7–12. How does Jesus's teaching here reflect the story of the paralyzed man? Think about that phrase "how much more." What did the paralyzed man initially want? What more did Jesus give him?

Read verse 12 again. How is this a call to courageous kindness? How did the four friends in Mark 2 live this out?

Think about the simple mechanics of four people carrying someone on a mat or stretcher. They literally had to bend low in order to lift him up. They saw their friend's distress and they wanted more for him— more life, more freedom, more hope. So they carried him where he could not get on his own. This is God's story for all of us!

Isaiah 63:9 says, "He redeemed them because of his love and compassion; he lifted them up and carried them all the days of the past." There's God's name on display again! He lifts us up and carries us when we can't go on. This is what Yahweh did for the Israelites. This is what Jesus does for all of us. And this is what He invites us to do for one another.

Bending low and lifting up is God's invitation to us as women of courageous kindness. Later this week and throughout the rest of this study, we'll look at how Jesus modeled this from His birth to His death. As we do, we'll discover that it's not just about our physical posture but the posture of our heart.

Right where you are, using exactly what you have, let humility, love, and compassion compel you to help carry someone today.

How have you experienced God's love and compassion through someone else bending low and lifting you up? In what ways do you need God to carry you today?

Look up Ephesians 4:1–2 and 1 Peter 3:8–9. How do these instructions inspire you to live out courageous kindness? How can you bend low and lift someone up this week?

Reflect on this prayer and make it your own today:

Yahweh, thank You for all the ways You put Your love and compassion on display. I want to be a woman who is willing to go beyond the minimum and live with bold, intentional kindness so that others might encounter You. Show me how. Lead the way. Amen.

Do nothing out of selfish ambition or vain conceit.
Rather, in humility value others above yourselves.

Philippians 2:3 NIV

After five years of prayer and working toward a God-given dream, I was ecstatic to be a cofounder of (in)courage, leading a new online space for women. It was a privilege to be at the forefront of what God was doing for His daughters. So I was shocked when just nine months after the launch of (in)courage, God asked me to move on to a new assignment He had for me and hand over my role to another.

After working so hard and waiting so long, I assumed that God would have me in this role for a long season. I thought, *I'm finally in the role God designed me for. I can settle in for at least the next five to ten years.*

But sometimes God's agenda is for us to loosen our grip and move on to the next step He has planned. And sometimes that means lifting someone else into the role we prayed and obeyed to secure. That's when I know I'm not doing my work with selfish ambition or vain conceit but in humility considering God's plan and another's interests above my own.

Helping someone else realize her dream by encouraging her, praying for her, and being available for her to process is a sweet gift. It was sometimes tempting to think I could do the job better, but that would be forgetting who is actually doing the work through me.

Paul writes, "For it is God who works in you to will and to act in order to fulfill his good purpose" (Phil. 2:13 NIV). God's good purpose doesn't hinge on our response, yet He delights in using us—through the power of the Holy Spirit—to bring about His plans.

What I've learned is that we need to be sensitive to God's leading, in both the big and the small things, so we can do what is best for the body of Christ and His kingdom even when it's hard. There are seasons to our individual callings in career and ministry. We do not own the role or gifting that God has given each of us. And sometimes that looks like giving our spot to another and helping a sister in Christ succeed for the sake of God's kingdom.

—STEPHANIE BRYANT

Why might God ask someone to give up what could be considered rightfully theirs in order to lift up another?

_____

_____

_____

_____

Yesterday we saw how a sister-in-law cleaned toilets and painted toenails to lift a pregnant mama's spirits and how a group of friends carried a paralyzed man to Jesus and changed his life forever. Today we'll see how bending low and lifting up isn't always an act of physical service but a posture of humility, encouragement, and kingdom-focused kindness.

Paul's letter to the Philippians shines a light on Jesus as the ultimate example of kindness. Chapter 2 begins with this exhortation: "Therefore if you have any encouragement from being united with Christ, if any comfort from his love, if any common sharing in the Spirit, if any tenderness and compassion, then make my joy complete by being like-minded, having the same love, being one in spirit and of one mind" (vv. 1–2 NIV).

Here Paul is setting up another if-then, cause-and-effect teaching. *If* we have experienced all of these things in Christ, *then* it ought to affect how we live. God's love is the central why and how of pursuing a life of courageous kindness.

> **God's love is the central why and how of pursuing a life of courageous kindness.**

Do you ever get tired of doing good? Have you grown weary of being kind and compassionate in a world that is competitive and divisive? Are you fed up with people who lack appreciation and respect? If humility and compassion feel out of reach, go back and remember who God is and what He's done for you.

Read Philippians 2:1–4. How do verses 1–2 prepare us to live out verses 3–4?

How is humility central to elevating the interests of others? List some examples of what valuing others above yourself might look like.

_____

_____

The next section of Paul's letter is where things get even juicier: "In your relationships with one another, have the same mindset as Christ Jesus" (v. 5 NIV). Before we examine what Jesus's mindset is, take a moment to remember that Jesus is an equal member of the triune God. "For the entire fullness of God's nature dwells bodily in Christ" (Col. 2:9). Since the beginning of time, Jesus was with God and He was God, and through Him everything was created (John 1:1–4). Any time we think and talk about Jesus, we must remember who He is and has always been—_God_. A heavenly, all-powerful being.

With this in mind, now read Philippians 2:5–11.

What was Jesus's attitude? List what He did that demonstrated that mindset.

_____

_____

_____

_____

What did God do because of Jesus's humility? Why do you think God chose a servant leadership approach to saving humanity (see vv. 9–11)?

_____

_____

_____

_____

Keep your Bible open to Philippians 2, because now we arrive at a wonderful word: *therefore*. "Therefore" tells us the *why* of all the *what* that preceded it. God's love and compassion, the Holy Spirit's guidance, Jesus's humble sacrifice to come to earth as a man and live and die for all humanity—*this* is our why. "Therefore, my dear friends, as you have always obeyed—not only in my presence, but now much more in my absence—continue to work out your salvation with fear and trembling, for it is God who works in you to will and to act in order to fulfill his good purpose" (vv. 12–13 NIV).

In other words, friend, keep going! Keep living in "responsive obedience" as The Message says in 2:12. Maybe God will ask you to surrender your comfortable church ministry in order to serve in a place that's floundering. Maybe at work you'll be asked to take a supporting role on a project so a coworker can shine. Maybe you'll keep doing kind things for your friend or neighbor that seemingly go unnoticed. Whatever it is, let God have full access to your heart, your mind, your life!

Jesus gave up everything that was rightfully His to be born in a stable, to battle storms and hunger and betrayal. He surrendered His own comfort and control to be obedient to the Father—a path that would lead to His brutal death on the cross. Why? Because living wasn't about Him. It was about us.

In our opening story, God asked Stephanie to relinquish her professional role to lift up someone else. What is God asking you to surrender today so that He might work through you (e.g., a job, a relationship, a possession, a spot on stage, a front-row seat)?

How can you courageously look to the interests of others this week?

Reflect on this prayer and make it your own today:

*Jesus, thank You for looking out for my interests, for valuing
me above Yourself. Please help me to do the same for others.
Show me today what it looks like to have a mindset like Yours.
Prepare my heart for responsive obedience—to lift up another
in partnership with Your good purposes. I trust You to work in
and through me. I'm Yours. Amen.*

When Moses's hands grew heavy, they took a stone and put it under him, and he sat down on it. Then Aaron and Hur supported his hands, one on one side and one on the other so that his hands remained steady until the sun went down.

Exodus 17:12

When God opened the door for me to attend graduate school and told me to walk through it, I didn't know whether to laugh or cry. I've always loved learning, and I knew that someday, when it made sense for me professionally and when the time was right for my family, I'd love to get a master's degree. But going back to school for an advanced English degree that had no clear career path when my boys were six, five, and three just didn't make sense. Plus I was also juggling working part-time from home (a job that was *not* the joy of my heart), leading in church ministry (which I did love), blogging regularly, and starting out as a public speaker—all of which made this *not* my idea of "the right time."

I was already drowning in my life, and everything I was doing felt essential. How could I possibly find the time and energy to do *more*?

Enter God. And enter Sara.

I wanted to obey God, so that meant trusting Him to take something off my plate or to expand my capacity—and He did both. But more than giving me supernatural energy to read complex literature and write lengthy term papers into the wee hours of the morning, God provided people to walk with me through grad school and to help carry my load. Sara was one of those people.

Her son, Mateo, was the same age as my youngest, Jude, and the two buds went to the same preschool two days a week. Sara and I set up a carpool system where I'd drop the boys off and she would pick them up. I cherished those quiet mornings—though three hours always flew by like lightning and I never got as much done as I had hoped.

But more often than not my phone would bing-bong and it would be a text from Sara: "We'd love to have Jude over for lunch today and play for a while if that's okay with you!"

"That would be wonderful. Thank you!" I'd text back, and then exhale with gratitude.

Sara was happy to have a playmate for her only child, but even more, my friend knew she was giving me the gift of time; she was helping me lean into what God had called me to do.

I never could have imagined the ways God used my three years of graduate school to set me on a path of work and ministry and writing beyond my dreams. Nor could I have imagined the countless hours (and meals, prayers, and words of encouragement) my friend Sara invested on my behalf along the way. I will never forget the way she sowed into my life with kindness and the great harvest it produced.

—BECKY KEIFE

Have you ever faced a seemingly impossible situation or season? How did God use other people to help you through that time?

Today we're going to hang out with our friend Moses again. Last week we read about how God provided manna for the Israelites as they wandered in the wilderness (Exod. 16). Immediately after that, we see God perform two more miracles that affirm two things: first, His kindness, compassion, and commitment to His people; and second, the fact that we're made to need one another.

At this point the Israelites have moved on from the Wilderness of Sin, where God first sent them food from heaven, to a place called Rephidim. And what is the first thing they start doing? Complaining. "We're thirsty. Give us water to drink. We were better off in Egypt."

God had miraculously filled their bellies every morning and every night. How could they forget?

Moses is understandably exasperated, so he cries out to God for help.

"What should I do with these people? In a little while they will stone me!" (Exod. 17:4).

Now, we know that God is on Moses's side. God had saved Moses as an infant from Pharaoh's edict to kill all Hebrew baby boys. He then called Moses out of Pharaoh's household and lit a fire of injustice in his heart to help rescue his true people from slavery. God helped Moses lead the Israelites out of Egypt by parting the Red Sea and delivering them safely on dry land. Clearly, God's favor has been upon him.

But the Israelites? With their constant whining, grumbling, and lack of trusting—shouldn't God be fed up with them by now?

Read Exodus 17:1–7. How does God answer Moses's plea for help? What does this tell you about how God feels and acts toward His people?

Like the Israelites, are you prone to forget what God has already done for you? Be honest. Write down your most common complaints. Next to each complaint, write down something true about who God is or how He has been faithful in the past.

Water from a rock to satisfy His people's thirst. Assurance of God's steadfast provision in every mouthwatering drop. This is God's first miracle in Exodus 17. And the miracle that comes next is even more of a life-and-death situation: the Israelites are under attack.

Moses sends Joshua and some handpicked men to fight the Amalekite army while he himself climbs a hill to view the battlefield. Moses tells the soldiers of Israel, "Tomorrow I will stand on the hilltop with God's staff in my hand" (v. 9). Pause and take note: this is the same staff that Moses lifted when God parted the Red Sea. The same staff that Moses struck on the rock to produce water.

Listen to what happens next:

> While Moses held up his hand, Israel prevailed, but whenever he put his hand down, Amalek prevailed. When Moses's hands grew heavy, they took a stone and put it under him, and he sat down on it. Then Aaron and Hur supported his hands, one on one side and one on the other so that his hands remained steady until the sun went down. So Joshua defeated Amalek and his army with the sword. (vv. 11–13)

Do you see? God called Moses to lead the Israelites, but He provided other people to help him along the way! Did Moses wield a sword in battle? No, Joshua did. Moses was tasked with raising his staff, the symbol of the Lord's power and strength. When his arms were up, Israel succeeded. But when Moses grew weary and the burden was too much to bear, did God say, "Oh well! Israel is doomed and my plans have been thwarted by your weakness"? No! Of course not. Aaron and Hur were there to lift Moses's hands for him.

God showed kindness to Moses and to Israel by sending support.

Read Exodus 17:8–16. What did God tell Moses to do once Amalek's army had been defeated? What's the significance of what Moses did right after that?

Think back over what you know from Scripture and from your own life experiences. When has the kindness of God been evident in how He used other people as support?

Do you ever wonder how Moses felt as his legs threatened to buckle and Aaron and Hur dragged a stone for him to sit on? What went through his mind as his arms wobbled and burned? His people's lives depended on his faltering strength. His courage must have increased as those two men came on either side and lifted his hands back up.

I don't know how Moses felt on that hill, but I know the thoughts that often went through my mind when I was facing the "battle" of graduate school: *It's your responsibility. Handle it on your own. Don't be a burden.* This is the voice of the world. Have you heard these messages too?

The world says, "Don't rely on others. Buck up and try harder. Needing people is weakness. You can only trust yourself. Don't bite off more than you can chew."

But God sings a different tune. God says, *Trust me; I will provide. You weren't meant to carry your burdens or your joys alone. I have wired you for community, connection, co-laboring, and collaboration. You will receive the greatest measure of My kindness when you walk most fully in obedience.*

Look up Psalm 37:23–24 and Psalm 94:18–19. What stands out to you from these verses? Where is God asking you to walk in obedience, trusting that He will provide what you need?

How can you be a Sara, a Joshua, or an Aaron and Hur to someone today? Who can you support in a practical way so they can accomplish what God has called them to do?

Reflect on this prayer and make it your own today:

God, You are a compassionate provider and a mighty miracle worker! Thank You for not turning Your back on me when I grumble and doubt. Grow in me a heart of trust and joyful obedience. Thank You for sending people to support me. Prepare me to help carry someone's burden, encourage their heart, or lift their hands today. May Your kindness shine through me. Amen.

As Jesus was walking along, he saw a man who had
been blind from birth. . . . Then he spit on the ground,
made mud with the saliva, and spread the mud over the
blind man's eyes.

John 9:1, 6 NLT

Our lunch trays were empty and it was time to return
to class. As my best friend and I turned the corner
toward the cafeteria window, I noticed a girl standing near
the trash cans—crying. I set down my tray and glanced
back at her, realizing it was my younger brother's best
friend.

I didn't know what to do. Should we ask her what was wrong, or
would drawing attention to her only embarrass her? Would she be
more upset if we stopped or if we kept walking? Had she even seen us?
Were we going to be late to class? I took a deep breath and walked up
to her. "Are you okay?" I asked gently.

She looked up and told us that she'd accidentally thrown away her
retainer with her lunch trash, and she just knew her parents would be
furious. My friend and I exchanged looks, and I'm pretty sure we felt
the same conflicting emotions at once: deep empathy and a desire to
help, as well as horror at the thought of what that help was going to
look like.

We looked into the trash can and realized it was nearly empty. Our
fears were confirmed when the cafeteria worker said yes, they'd just
taken bags of trash out to the dumpster. She reluctantly pointed to the

door that led outside and shrugged when we asked if we could look through the discarded bags.

Slowly but with determination, we walked outside and faced down that smelly bin of waste. We took a deep breath (and then regretted it!) and opened a bag. Then another and another and another, until we reached the last bag of that day's nasty, smelly, slimy lunch trash. And that was when we found it.

The retainer—and our young friend—was rescued! After wading through the muck together, we really did feel triumphant. We also reeked of foods that should never be combined and that should never be seen again after being thrown into a trash can.

We were now extremely late to class, though we suspected someone had probably told our teachers where we'd been. We'd certainly caught the attention of plenty of passing students when we searched the trash can inside and talked to the lunch lady. And now we were filthy—and facing a long walk of smelly shame back to class.

But as a girl once again in possession of her retainer gushed gratitude at us and then rushed back to her class, my friend and I exchanged another look and a chuckle. What we'd just done was *not* fun, but we'd done it together—and helping someone was worth it. And I'm pretty sure neither one of us ever ate school lunch again.

—MARY CARVER

Have you ever said yes to helping with an unpleasant task? What does it require to put someone else's need above your own comfort?

Don't you just love Mary's honesty as she describes her "deep empathy and a desire to help, as well as horror at the thought of what that help was going to look like"? Haven't we all felt that way at some point when weighing our wish to show love and kindness against the discomfort it's going to cost us? The battle of our flesh is real. But when the battle rages, when we're looking at our own metaphorical school cafeteria trash can and wondering if we should dive in, we need only remember that Jesus was the original dumpster diver and that He calls us to join Him.

Okay, so maybe Scripture doesn't actually show Jesus digging through trash, but it certainly shows Him getting dirty in order to love people.

We find one of many such moments in John 9 when Jesus comes across a man who was born blind. Jesus's disciples want to know the cause of the man's blindness—did the man sin or his parents? "'Neither this man nor his parents sinned,' Jesus answered. 'This came about so that God's works might be displayed in him'" (v. 3).

Jesus proceeds to spit on the ground, make mud from His saliva, and spread it on the man's eyes. Then Jesus told him to go wash in the pool of Siloam. The man obeyed and came back seeing (vv. 6–7).

Read John 9:1–11. How did this moment begin? (Hint, look at verse 1.) What does this tell you about opportunities to demonstrate courageous kindness?

What hinders you from seeing someone and responding to their needs as you're passing by?

_____

_____

_____

_____

When reading a story in the Bible, it's important to look at the larger context. Ask yourself questions like, What happened right before or after this incident? How is this story part of the greater narrative or teaching?

In this instance, a quick look back at John 8 shows that right before Jesus passed by the blind man, He had been in the temple teaching the Jews about the freedom that comes from believing in Him (vv. 31–36). This occurred right after Jesus halted the stoning of the woman caught in adultery (vv. 1–11). Sounds like Jesus is an impressive guy, right? But Jesus's radical teaching about freedom, forgiveness, and loving the One whom the Father sent was met with extreme resistance. The Jews accused Jesus of having a demon and doubted His every word (vv. 52–53).

This is what led up to the final words in John 8: "So they picked up stones to throw at him. But Jesus was hidden and went out of the temple" (v. 59).

Why is this context important? Because the very next thing that John records are these now familiar words: "As he was passing by, he saw a man blind from birth" (John 9:1).

Do you see what this means? Even after a full day of ministry and a heated debate, even after engaging with difficult people and fearing for His own safety, Jesus was still living with eyes wide open to the people around Him. As He was going on His way, Jesus was actively surrendered to loving people "so that God's works might be displayed" (9:3).

Picture the scene from John 9 again. Jesus spitting on the ground, then bending low to mix His saliva with dirt until it formed a muddy paste that He scooped up and spread on the blind man's eyes. Now read Psalm 40:1–3. What comparisons can you draw between these two pictures?

_____

_____

_____

_____

In these two passages, what is the result when someone experiences the kindness of God?

_____

_____

_____

_____

As I go on my way, Lord, have your way with me.

This is our simple difference, courageous kindness prayer. While they didn't use these exact words, Mary Carver (from our opening story) and Jesus both lived out this prayer. Mary was on her way to class when she noticed a distraught student. She was willing to bend low into the filth of school cafeteria garbage to lift up the plight and concerns of another. Jesus was passing by after leaving the temple when He observed a blind man and bent low to heal him.

As I go on my way, Lord, have your way with me.

This is how God asks us to live out courageous kindness too.

It takes courage to put aside our own interests and agendas—whether that's being on time to class, escaping from an angry mob, or more likely something in between.

It takes courage to get dirty. The stench of the dumpster stayed with Mary and her friend all afternoon at school. And imagine the way Jesus's skin remained stained by the mud as He went about His day, the creases of His hands lined dark with the earthy reminder of meeting someone in their need. The same will be true for you. You will be marked by your kindness—and so will the person you were kind to.

Read the remainder of Psalm 40. What stands out to you about God's character and His heart for you?

_____

_____

_____

_____

How does the psalmist David respond to God's faithfulness? How can this give you courage to bend low in love as you go on your way this week?

_____

_____

_____

_____

Reflect on this prayer and make it your own today:

Oh, Jesus, sometimes I'm like the blind man and the retainer girl, stuck in my predicament and losing hope. Other times I'm *like Mary, looking at someone who needs help, trying to decide if I'm willing to bend low and get dirty. Lord, help me in both scenarios. Grow my faith to believe that Your love and kindness can reach into my current circumstances. And then grow in me a heart of surrender so that I may choose courageous kindness as I go on my way today. Amen.*

Older women are to . . . teach what is good, so that they may encourage the young women.

Titus 2:3–4

As someone who grew up with almost no motherly influence, I have a strong desire for older women in my life. God has answered that longing through many different people, including my former pastor's wife, DeLynn. DeLynn is smart, creative, talented, and encouraging. She has loved Jesus her whole life and is the picture of Southern style and grace—and she's also kind of feisty. Her encouragement has a lot of action behind it.

That's exactly the type of encouragement I need. I have big, God-sized dreams that scare me. Too often I lose sight of the gifts God has given me. Fear grips me more times than I care to admit. I fear failure. I fear success. It all makes fulfilling God's call on my life that much harder.

DeLynn, on the other hand, is wise, passionate, and brave in all of the ways I'm not. I can think back on several occasions when I sat in her kitchen and wept over my hurt and fear and confusion. Every time she looked me in the eye and reminded me who God is and what His promises are. She never let me drown in my tears. She never let me wallow in self-pity for too long.

During my greatest moments of doubt, she believed in me and for me. She proved her confidence in me time and time again. My weakness never deterred her. It may have actually made her lean in more.

She took her role seriously as mama of the house. She didn't consider herself better than those she was leading. She didn't abuse her position in the church. She leveraged it for those of us wanting to learn and grow in Jesus and in ministry.

DeLynn opened doors for me by giving me many opportunities to exercise my gifts and talents, but more importantly, she challenged me and pushed me out of my comfort zone. She helped me find my brave.

—KARINA ALLEN

How is God's nature reflected in our need for meaningful and nurturing relationships?

_____

_____

_____

_____

We were designed with an innate longing to be mothered and fathered, to be mentored, encouraged, spurred on, and protected. As God's very nature is relational—Father, Son, and Spirit coexisting as one—so as His image bearers our hearts are created for relationship.

It is by God's design that we bend low to help each other in times of hardship and lift one another up.

What good news this is! To know that our desire—our _need_—to do life with others and have people come alongside us is God-given.

It is by His design that we bend low to help each other in times of hardship and lift one another up to fulfill our purpose.

Karina's story beautifully illustrates a Titus 2 woman: "Older women are to be reverent in behavior, not slanderers, not slaves to excessive drinking. They are to teach what is good, so that they may encourage the young women to love their husbands and to love their children, to be self-controlled, pure, workers at home, kind, and in submission to their husbands, so that God's word will not be slandered" (vv. 3–5).

Now, Karina is a single woman, so does DeLynn's influence in her life not apply because her encouragement isn't centered around motherhood and marriage? Of course not! The heart of Paul's message is the importance of those farther along in life and faith helping those who are a few steps behind—passing on their wisdom and sowing encouragement in their hearts.

Read 1 Thessalonians 2:7–12. What imagery of a family does Paul use? What does this tell you about the way we are wired to need one another?

Write out verses 11–12 in your own words. Who in your life can you care for in this way?

"Encouraging, comforting, and urging you to live lives worthy of God" (v. 11 NIV). Yes, isn't that what we all need? It is through this kind of encouragement and support from one another that we will be able to live a life of courageous kindness and make a difference right where we are. We weren't meant to do it alone.

In Titus 3:1–2, Paul has additional instructions for how we ought to live out our faith shoulder to shoulder with our brothers and sisters. He starts off with a list of reminders:

- Submit to authority
- Obey
- Be ready for every good work
- Slander no one
- Avoid fighting
- Be kind
- Always show gentleness to all people

Sounds pretty good, right? But simple instructions can be complicated to live out.

Read Titus 3:1–2. Which thing(s) on Paul's list is most challenging for you to live out and why? How can you courageously address that area in your life until it aligns with Scripture?

Continue reading in Titus 3:4–8. What did God reveal (or cause to appear, depending on your translation)? What did God pour out on us?

Are your mental wheels spinning? Are the dots of Scripture connecting? Over and over the Bible repeats God's offer, provision, and invitation.

The offer: God's love, kindness, and mercy.

The provision: Jesus's perfect life and death, and the guiding Holy Spirit.

The invitation: Share the love and goodness you've received.

In the short passage we just read, we see again the powerful words *so that*. "He poured out his Spirit on us abundantly through Jesus Christ our Savior *so that*, having been justified by his grace, we may become heirs with the hope of eternal life" (vv. 6–7).

Maybe today you're longing for a mother figure or father figure. Maybe you yearn for a friend or mentor to make space for your tears and fears while showing you God's love and helping you find your brave. That is a good desire. In fact, God has already answered that longing from an eternal perspective. God has *abundantly* given you His Spirit. Why? *So that* you may be an heir, a child of God with the steadfast hope of spending eternity with your heavenly Father.

Paul continues in verse 8, "This saying is trustworthy. I want you to insist on these things, *so that* those who have believed God might be careful to devote themselves to good works. These are good and profitable for everyone."

This is the crux of why we're doing this study. We lean into Scripture, we study God's Word, and we apply His instructions *so that* we can do the good things God wants us to do!

How would you summarize God's call from today's study to be a woman of courageous kindness?

_____

_____

_____

_____

Read Titus 3:14. Ask God to show you someone who has an urgent need that you can help to meet. Write it down, and then come back and record what happened when you bent low to lift up another.

_____

_____

_____

_____

Reflect on this prayer and make it your own today:

_God, thank You for loving me and creating me for relationship—
with You and with others. Not only do I not want to do life
on my own, but I can't do it. I need You, and I need spiritual
mothers and fathers and sisters in Christ. Please provide the
encouragement and support I need today, and show me opportunities to extend this love and kindness to others. Amen._

> **For a deeper look at this week's study and to spur on discussion if you're working with a small group, watch a FREE video from (in)courage at incourage.me/biblestudy.**

WEEK 4

compassion and inconvenience

"What do you think? Which of the three became a neighbor to the man attacked by robbers?"

"The one who treated him kindly," the religion scholar responded.

Jesus said, "Go and do the same."

Luke 10:36–37 MSG

I was about to cook my first turkey dinner for Thanksgiving. It felt like a big deal. I had no idea how to cook a turkey, but I figured if most people managed to cook a turkey on Thanksgiving, I could somehow figure out how to cook the bird myself.

I'd bought all the groceries I needed—far too many potatoes, if I'm being honest, but I've always been a firm believer in having as many mashed potatoes as possible.

I decided to cook at my sister's house because she has a bigger kitchen, so I lugged all my groceries from the fridge in my apartment down to my car. It took three trips. On my final trip down, turkey tucked safely in my arms, I noticed the door of my neighbor's apartment had water seeping out beneath it.

I kept walking, noticing more and more water filling the hallway. I sighed and looked down at the turkey I was holding. I was on a strict timeline—I had even drafted an oven schedule so I'd know exactly what time everything should be cooking.

My neighbor popped out from behind her door, looking frantic. "There's water everywhere!"

She wasn't speaking to me, exactly, but there was no one else in the hallway. For a split second, I considered continuing on my way and pretending I hadn't seen her. But then I remembered a prayer I'd prayed only days earlier: *God, give me opportunities to meet my neighbors.*

I wanted to laugh. God sure answered that prayer quickly! So I stopped and introduced myself. "I'm Aliza. I can help. Do you have a mop?"

"I'm Mara," she said.

Mara and I talked as we mopped. More accurately, I did the mopping and she did the talking. I couldn't help but smile, though. I briefly whispered a prayer to God and told Him, *Thanks for the chance to meet Mara. Maybe this is exactly what Thanksgiving is for.*

Mara and I didn't become best friends, but we did exchange Christmas cards, and now we smile wider when we see each other in the hallway.

My turkey dinner was a little late. But as the day passed and I was able to start cooking, I became more and more grateful for my encounter with Mara. And I started to wonder: perhaps being inconvenienced is actually the best way to love your neighbor.

—ALIZA LATTA

What would you do if you saw an opportunity to help someone but it would be a big inconvenience? Would you pretend not to see their need and rush by, or would you "put down your turkey"?

When we think about courageous, "as we go on our way" kindness, it's easy to want to look at it through a shiny Instagram filter. As in, how nice to hold the door for a hands-full mama as you walk into a store. Or how kind to pick up the tab for the person behind you in the drive-through line. Sure, such small gestures are great and will probably put a smile on someone's face—maybe even assure them that a total stranger (and God) is mindful of them.

But this week we're going to discover that while courageous kindness can be simple, it also requires our *compassion* and *inconvenience*. That first word might sound warm and fuzzy, but the second . . . not so much. However, as we'll learn today in a story Jesus told to a group of religious leaders, we can't truly *live* without either.

The scene begins in Luke 10:25 when an expert of the law tried to test Jesus by asking, "Teacher, what must I do to inherit eternal life?" Jesus replied by turning it back on the expert: "What is written in the law? How do you read it?" (v. 26).

The man answered by quoting from the law of Moses: "'Love the Lord your God with all your heart, with all your soul, with all your strength, and with all your mind,' and '[love] your neighbor as yourself'" (v. 27).

Courageous kindness requires our compassion and inconvenience.

Jesus affirmed the man's answer was correct. "Do this and you will live," he replied (v. 28).

But the religious leader wasn't satisfied. He wanted to justify his actions and beliefs, so he asked, "And who is my neighbor?" (v. 29).

In other words, the guy was looking for a loophole.

Think about your own tendency to look for loopholes or fit obedience to God into a comfortable box—one that might preclude you from, say, picking up a mop. Write an honest list of barriers that keep you from loving others.

Read Luke 10:25–37 to find Jesus's full response to the question "Who is my neighbor?" What stands out to you from the parable of the good Samaritan?

Surely the man questioning Jesus and the two Jewish men in the story who passed by on the other side knew God's command to love your neighbor. But Jesus's parable makes clear that they were lacking two things: compassion and a correctly applied definition of being a neighbor.

The Greek word translated as "neighbor" is *plesion*, which is a general term "expressing the idea of one's fellow human being."[1] Easy, right? This is how most of us today would also view the term. But as one commentary explains, "The lawyer's question is really an attempt to create a distinction, arguing that some people are neighbors and others are not, and that one's responsibility is only to love God's people. The suggestion that some people are 'non-neighbors' is what Jesus responds to in his story."[2]

From a present-day perspective, we can be quick to wag a mental finger at the religious teacher and his seemingly self-serving query. We know that God loves *all* people. But before Christ, there was no *all*. There were God's people (the Jews) and everybody else (the Gentiles). Neighbor and non-neighbor. Jesus changed that. He demonstrated through His life and ultimately His death that we are one humanity and that relationships trump religiosity.

Eternal life is not about upholding laws but loving people.

Read Romans 13:8–10. How would you summarize Paul's teaching?

_____

_____

_____

_____

Technically, the priest and the Levite who passed by the wounded man did him no wrong. They weren't the ones who beat and robbed him, right? But in view of how Jesus describes being a neighbor (see Luke 10:36–37), how are we to explain Paul's statement that "love does no wrong" (Rom. 13:10)?

_____

_____

_____

_____

_____

"But a Samaritan on his journey came up to him, and when he saw the man, he had compassion" (Luke 10:33). *On his journey . . . he had compassion.* Don't you love that? As he was on his way, the traveler saw a need and chose to respond with kindness—even at his own inconvenience. Mr. Samaritan could basically be our *Courageous Kindness* poster child.

The Greek word translated as "compassion" is *splanchnizomai*, which can also be translated as "pity." This is not just some warm, fuzzy feeling; *splanchnizomai* is a verb that means to be deeply moved with compassion. In our opening story, Aliza was moved with compassion to set down the turkey and her carefully planned Thanksgiving dinner timetable to pick up a mop and help her neighbor.

Likewise, the Samaritan did not simply feel sorry for the beaten man. He didn't just think, *Oh, that's a shame*, or, *Bad break for that guy*, or even, *I hope he doesn't suffer too long*. No, his compassion compelled him to action. He cleaned and bandaged the man's wounds. He put the battered man on his donkey, took him to an inn, and paid for his care (vv. 34–35).

Do you think this was part of the Samaritan's plan when he started his day? Of course not. It was a total inconvenience. It cost him time and money. It likely had implications for his job and family. And yet it's beautifully clear that the Samaritan loved in the way he would want someone to love him.

Loving our neighbor starts with *being* a neighbor. It's not how we classify others but how we choose to love. We all belong to one another because we all belong to God. This is our call to courageous kindness, our charge to change the world by being a neighbor who shows compassion even when it inconveniences us.

When has someone loved you with compassion in action? Record that experience here and give thanks for it.

_____

_____

_____

_____

How can you apply today's teaching and live out God's call to courageous kindness?

_____

_____

_____

_____

Reflect on this prayer and make it your own today:

Jesus, if there is any way I have falsely understood who my neighbor is, please correct my thinking. As You extend love and compassion to all people, I want to do the same. Lord, give me an opportunity this week to be a neighbor to someone. I'm willing to be inconvenienced for Your name's sake. Amen.

I have compassion on the crowd.

Mark 8:2

Several years ago I watched from afar as a dear friend from college battled breast cancer. When Alyssa was diagnosed, she had a toddler the same age as one of my sons and was expecting baby number two. Even though I hadn't seen Alyssa in years, I cried when I saw photos of her bald head and pregnant belly. I chipped in with friends to send a care package. And I prayed.

I often shared Alyssa's Facebook posts and invited others to pray with me when she was having surgery, starting another round of chemo, or delivering her baby. In this way, several friends who had never met Alyssa became invested in her story too.

So when the news came that Alyssa was cancer-free, my friends rejoiced with me!

And then when the cancer came back—widespread and aggressive—many in my community mourned too. Less than five months after her second diagnosis, Alyssa left the pain of this world and entered the arms of Jesus. In the midst of overwhelming grief, I also had the overwhelming desire to go to Alyssa's memorial service—to bear witness to the world's profound loss and celebrate the light Alyssa shined.

It wasn't easy finding a way to go out of town and leave three littles during my husband's busiest work and travel season. But eventually I lined up a couple different people to help. Then, two days before I was set to leave, one of my helpers got the stomach flu. I had no backup childcare. No one else who could step in. I was devastated.

The next day I was at church when my friend Shannon asked how I was doing and if I was going to the funeral. Shannon didn't know Alyssa but had been following along through Facebook and regularly prayed for my sweet friend and her young family.

I told Shannon how I had really hoped to go but my childcare plans fell through. I couldn't hold back the tears. Shannon handed me a tissue from her purse and without skipping a beat said, "Maybe I can watch the boys for you. I'll have to double-check if I can move a couple things around, but I should be able to do it."

Shannon had never watched my kids before. We honestly weren't super close at the time. Yet here she was, rearranging her schedule to help. I couldn't believe someone would do that for me.

As I traveled the long stretch of California highway to Alyssa's funeral, a steady stream of tears coursed down my cheeks. Yes, I grieved my beautiful friend's passing, but I also cried for another beautiful friend's outpouring of compassion. A kindness I will never forget.

—BECKY KEIFE

When has someone's compassion surprised you? What effect did their kindness have on you?

By now we know that God is compassionate, and Jesus lived out that compassion during His time on earth. And yet, sometimes Jesus's actions can still make us do a double take—like in Mark 8 when He feeds four thousand people. No, that's not a typo. The story is so similar to the one we looked at back in week 2, when Jesus fed five thousand hungry men plus women and children with just five loaves and two fish.

But the story in Mark 8 brings us to a different day, a different place, and a different crowd. With the same Jesus.

> He called the disciples and said to them, "I have compassion on the crowd, because they've already stayed with me three days and have nothing to eat. If I send them home hungry, they will collapse on the way, and some of them have come a long distance." (vv. 1–3)

There's that word again! Compassion. *Splanchnizomai.* The same word used in Luke 10:33 to describe how the Samaritan reacted to the wounded man. A feeling that provokes an action. This is how Jesus consistently sees people and responds.

The disciples are also (woefully) consistent. Again, they question Jesus about the logistics of being so compassionate. "Where can anyone get enough bread here in this desolate place to feed these people?" (Mark 8:4). Never mind that they had already seen how Jesus could feed a large crowd with a small meal.

Do the disciples ever remind you of the Israelites in the desert when they questioned how God would satisfy their thirst right after He had been faithful to satisfy their hunger? Maybe we're not so unlike them.

How are you prone to forget what God has already done? How would remembering His past faithfulness fuel your faith today?

_____

_____

Read Psalm 107. (It's long but worth it.) Note how many times the psalmist repeats the phrases "give thanks" and "he saved them from their distress." (Your translation might say "rescued" or "delivered.") What does this repetition tell you about God's character and how we ought to respond?

_____

_____

_____

_____

_____

Returning our attention to the hungry crowd, Jesus asks the doubtful disciples, "How many loaves do you have?" (Mark 8:5). This time the disciples had seven.

> He commanded the crowd to sit down on the ground. Taking the seven loaves, he gave thanks, broke them, and gave them to his disciples to set before the people. So they served them to the crowd. They also had a few small fish, and after he had blessed them, he said these were to be served as well. They ate and were satisfied. Then they collected seven large baskets of leftover pieces. (vv. 6–8)

What did Jesus do with the loaves in His hand? *He gave thanks.*

Before there was enough food to pass out, before the need was met and bellies were filled, Jesus took what was available, what was already provided, and gave thanks.

Where the disciples saw only the immediate predicament, Jesus saw the possibility of God's power.

Where are you in need today? How could you shift your focus from what you lack to what God has already provided?

_____

_____

_____

_____

_____

Read Psalm 111. What recurring truths or themes stand out to you? Write down a couple lines of your own praise back to God.

_____

_____

_____

_____

_____

In the opening story, I had put my hope in my own abilities to orchestrate childcare, trusting that my effort would produce the result I desired. When my plans fell through, all I saw was my predicament. But so did God. He heard my cries and was moved with compassion. Where I felt like hope was lost, God was ready to use what He had already provided through my friend Shannon.

First John 3:16–18 says, "This is how we have come to know love: He laid down his life for us. We should also lay down our lives for our brothers and sisters. If anyone has this world's goods and sees a fellow believer in need but withholds compassion from him—how does God's love reside in him? Little children, let us not love in word or speech, but in action and in truth."

> "Let us not love in word or speech, but in action and in truth." (1 John 3:18)

It was in Shannon's power to help, so she did. It cost her the inconvenience of rearranging her schedule and pouring out energy and attention on two spirited little boys. But Shannon loved me in action— reminding me again of the truth of God's endless compassion.

May we be women of courageous kindness too. Ready to pray, ask someone how they're doing, offer a tissue, and give the gift of our compassion and inconvenience.

What does it mean to you to "lay down our lives for our brothers and sisters"?

Read John 15:13. How can you courageously live this kind of love today?

Reflect on this prayer and make it your own today:

Jesus, thank You for having compassion on the hungry crowd and on me. Help me focus less on my predicaments and more on what You've already provided; less on my own plans and more on Your power. And give me opportunities this week to tangibly love others. Thank You for laying down Your life for me. Prepare me to do the same for my friends. Amen.

Come to me, all of you who are weary and burdened,
and I will give you rest.

Matthew 11:28

I'll be honest, I don't like to be inconvenienced. I often
have a one-track mind. When I'm on task, I keep my eyes
straight ahead, rarely veering to the right or left. This way
of operating keeps me getting stuff done, but it also keeps
me from seeing some of the needs around me.

I also don't like to be the person who inconveniences others—
probably because for most of my life no one wanted to be inconvenienced by me. I didn't grow up with a traditional family, and in many
ways, I had to raise myself. I've lived on my own since I was seventeen.
I've learned to be independent and to make do with what I have. I make
my own way, I make my own choices, and I meet my own needs.

But then came Jesus. He changed a lot of that. And He is continuing
to teach me who He is as my provider, my comforter, and my friend.
When you're used to doing everything on your own, it's hard to believe
there's another way. But He's growing me.

Being dependent on God is one thing, but being dependent on others
to some extent feels even harder. I don't tend to ask for help until I've
exhausted all of my options. I don't make my needs known because I
never want to be a burden on others.

God has used a recurring struggle in my life to remind me that my
needs are not a burden to Him or to others: car woes. I've had car

troubles more times than I care to count. During one long stretch of time when I was sadly between cars, I was embarrassed about my situation and also embarrassed to ask for help. But God asked me to practice humility and set aside my pride. So I did it. I asked for help. It was all kinds of hard.

But when I asked, my friend Sharika answered. She had a super intense job that required her to work long hours, but she loved me and wanted to help me. Day after day, she would either take me to work or pick me up and bring me home. She helped me repeatedly for weeks and weeks.

It probably wasn't a big deal to her, but to me it meant everything. She went out of her way to show up and tangibly be the hands and feet of Jesus in my life. God did a work in both of us, and we are better friends to each other and to others because of it.

—KARINA ALLEN

Do you struggle with telling your needs to others because you fear you'll be a burden? Where do you think that fear comes from?

_____

_____

_____

_____

Here's the deal, friend. If Jesus continually set an example of laying down His life for His friends—through daily compassion, inconvenience, and the ultimate sacrifice—_and_ He continually asks us to love others like He did, then we have to accept (and expect!) that sometimes we will be the ones on the receiving end of that love.

Look back at the passage we read at the end of our study yesterday. "This is how we have come to know love: He laid down his life for us. We should also lay down our lives for our brothers and sisters. If anyone has this world's goods and sees a fellow believer in need but withholds compassion from him—how does God's love reside in him? Little children, let us not love in word or speech, but in action and in truth" (1 John 3:16–18).

Zoom in on that phrase "sees a fellow believer in need." What does this presume? That people will have needs!

We are all people, friend—including you.

Whether you've been forced to be independent since childhood, like Karina, or you've been burned or let down by friends as an adult—or you're just afraid you might be—it's easy to want to be the one who holds it all together. Sometimes we're even willing to do the holding for someone else without believing we are also worthy of being held.

Read what Jesus says in Matthew 11:28–30. What are Jesus's first three words? Receive His words as a personal invitation to you, and then write down what burdens you're carrying right now.

What does Jesus promise to give us? What does He ask us to do?

"Come to me, all of you who are weary and burdened." Jesus doesn't say that we should not be weary or that we should fix our burdens before we come. He doesn't invite just a few people who are weary because of special circumstances. We find no judgment or condition in His words. Rather, Jesus offers an all-call invitation to His people whom He *expects* to be burdened and weary.

God isn't surprised by your broken-down car or broken relationship. He's not upset that you feel depleted in your career or in your parenting, or that your pocketbook is empty. Because Jesus chose to cloak Himself in humanity, He knows in a parched-mouth, tired-muscles, broken-heart kind of way how wearisome and burdensome being a person can be.

This is why He came to earth and why He keeps opening His arms, asking us to come to Him.

Look up Mark 10:13–16. How does Jesus respond to the children? What do you think Jesus means by receiving the kingdom of God like a little child?

As you consider your own needs, how does Jesus's posture toward children affect the way you view your own dependency?

Like a loving father with a young child, God sees our limitations and responds with compassion and provision. Similarly, the Bible is also full of imagery that depicts God as a shepherd who cares for His sheep. For example, in the Old Testament we find passages like Isaiah 40:11: "He tends his flock like a shepherd: He gathers the lambs in his arms and carries them close to his heart; he gently leads those that have young" (NIV).

> **Like a loving father with a young child, God sees our limitations and responds with compassion and provision.**

Then all through the Gospels we hear Jesus's own words, like in John 10:14–15, where He says, "I am the good shepherd; I know my sheep and my sheep know me—just as the Father knows me and I know the Father— and I lay down my life for the sheep."

As we close today's study, let's soak in the truth that we are God's sheep—often weak and vulnerable and in need, but always known and held by our Good Shepherd. And when we listen to His voice, we'll also hear Him calling us to join Him in caring for His flock.

To answer that call is to live as women of courageous kindness.

After Jesus died on the cross and rose again, He appeared to His disciples and gave them final instructions. Read John 21:15–19. What does Jesus repeatedly tell Peter to do? What are His last two words in verse 19?

The world might tell you to buck up and handle life on your own. But God designed us to be beautifully dependent on Him and on one another. How will you courageously choose to come to the Shepherd and also help feed His sheep today?

Reflect on this prayer and make it your own today:

God, thank You that I don't have to fix my problems or clean myself up before coming to You. Help me to learn from You— both to receive the compassion and rest You offer and to show compassion and sacrificial love to others. I need You, Lord, and I'm ready to be used by You. Amen.

For where two or three are gathered together in my
name, I am there among them.

Matthew 18:20

A t some point during our drive south on I-75, the
trees change. Spanish moss hangs from branches
like an old lady's forgotten shawl. We sit in the cab of a
small U-Haul, driving our belongings to a new home for the
year.

My body aches as the truck bumps forward, carrying us to a new
state and a new community as we get closer to our son's due date. I rub
my belly, wondering how long these haunting feelings of fear and loneliness will chase us. The moss starts to look less like shawls and more
like ghosts.

That year—the year we moved to Florida, the year after we moved
back to the States from living overseas—I felt more foreign than I ever
had before. It was also the year I met Anita.

Anita and her family moved to Orlando at the same time we did, and
we became fast friends. She was the kind of person who looked you so
deep in the eyes with kindness when she spoke, that you immediately
felt loved, welcomed, and wholly received.

A few short months after moving, Anita shared the news that she
was expecting. We sat on a bench and prayed for the new life growing
inside of her, and for the new life growing inside of me that we were
about to welcome into the world.

And then, only weeks before my son was due, Anita texted and asked me to meet her at the bench where we often prayed. She rubbed a charm from her necklace between her fingers and told me that there was no heartbeat at their last appointment. We cried and sat in silence together. My pregnant belly never felt larger and heavier than it did while sitting beside her in that moment.

On the day my son arrived, Anita was at the same hospital for a D&C. I lay there thinking about the irony. I wondered how our friendship would change. I expected it would. If the tables were turned, I would've distanced myself from her. But a few hours later, Anita was standing in the doorway. She and her husband found our room before heading to hers. She prayed over my fears and looked me deep in the eyes with love.

In her own suffering, Anita drew near and put my feelings ahead of her own. And to this day, more than ten years later, it leaves me undone and leads me. She was the hands, face, and voice of Christ, who came near with a depth I'd only known before by reading Scripture. She upended my expectation to be haunted by fear and foreignness. Her kindness shook the ghosts away.

—TASHA JUN

What thoughts, longings, or memories does Tasha's story stir for you?

One of the greatest expressions of God's compassion toward His people is being available. From walking in the garden with Adam and

Eve, to meeting Moses on Mount Sinai, to taking on flesh and traveling with a band of ragtag disciples, God has made Himself available to His people.

Tasha's story about her friendship with Anita beautifully captures three ways God expresses the kindness of availability: in acceptance, in presence, and in prayer.

After moving to a new state, Tasha was desperate to be known, seen, and accepted just as she was. Tasha describes Anita as "the kind of person who looked you so deep in the eyes with kindness when she spoke, that you immediately felt loved, welcomed, and wholly received." Guess who else is that kind of person? Jesus.

When Jesus looked at the woman caught in adultery, He didn't see an imprint of a scarlet letter *A*; He saw the imprint of His own image (John 8:3–11). When Jesus looked at ten men with leprosy, He didn't see a disease; He saw friends longing to be free (Luke 17:11–19). When Jesus spoke with the Samaritan woman at the well, He didn't see a person of a lesser class, race, or status. He didn't even see someone marked by a lifetime of bad choices. He saw a thirsty daughter in need of living water (John 4:1–26).

Read John 4:1–26. What was the woman's first response to Jesus engaging with her? What things about yourself cause you to put up relational barriers or expect *not* to be accepted by God or others?

What does Jesus's promise in verses 13–14 say about when and how He's making Himself available?

_____

_____

_____

_____

_____

We started this whole study with the foundational truth of Romans 5:8, "But God proves his own love for us in that while we were still sinners, Christ died for us." Do you see how this is crucial to our understanding of God's compassion and learning to follow Him in a life of courageous kindness? God doesn't make us first prove ourselves worthy of relationship; He accepts us just as we are—broken and sinful and messy—and He says, "Come know Me and be known by Me."

Just as God accepts us and offers His steadfast presence—through the life and death of Jesus, through the counsel of the Holy Spirit, and ultimately through eternal life with Him in heaven—so we are called to see and accept others as God's beloved sons and daughters. The gift of our presence shouldn't hinge on someone's external beauty, desirable circumstances, or what we can get in return.

> **Sometimes the greatest kindness we can offer is just being willing to show up.**

Like with Tasha and Anita, sometimes the greatest kindness we can offer is just being willing to show up. To sit together on a bench and rejoice when there's reason to celebrate and grieve when there's reason to mourn (Rom. 12:15). Surely life is full of both.

Proverbs 17:17 says, "A friend loves at all times, and a brother is born for a difficult time." Who has been that kind of friend in your life? What did the kindness of their presence mean to you?

_____

_____

_____

_____

Look up Exodus 3:12. What did God say to Moses when he was worried about leading the Israelites out of Egypt? Then read Joshua 1:5. What did God say to Joshua before he led the Israelites into the promised land? Where in your life do you need assurance of God's presence?

_____

_____

_____

_____

When Tasha felt alone in a new place and scared to become a new mom, God used Anita to comfort and encourage her through the gifts of acceptance, presence, and prayer. Even during her own pain, Anita's compassion for her friend moved her to pray.

Prayer is the most tender and powerful way we are invited to connect deeply with God and others. In Matthew 18:20 Jesus promises, "For where two or three are gathered together in my name, I am there among them."

Hebrews 4:16 tells us, "Therefore, let us approach the throne of grace with boldness, so that we may receive mercy and find grace to help us in time of need." Anita wasn't timid about lavishing Tasha with compassion and taking her needs to God. Her kindness was courageous. She trusted God to pour out His compassion on her own broken heart, and she trusted Him to give her strength to keep on loving her friend.

Indeed, the kindness of God is the kindness we can extend to others.

Look up James 5:16 and Romans 8:26–27. What is our role in praying for one another? What does God promise to do on our behalf?

How is God asking you to love someone with your acceptance, presence, and prayer this week?

Reflect on this prayer and make it your own today:

God, thank You for accepting me, being present with me, and even intervening in prayer for me. Truly Your kindness and compassion are evident throughout Scripture and in my own life. Please help me to share with others all the kindness I've received from You. Give me opportunities this week to simply be available for another in their time of need. Amen.

Each of you should use whatever gift you have received
to serve others, as faithful stewards of God's grace in its
various forms.

1 Peter 4:10 NIV

I've been traveling with my family to Haiti for almost two decades now. Each trip is full of opportunities to listen and learn, to be challenged and inspired. Our trip last summer was no exception. I was slated to speak at the Esther Women's Conference for three churches in the northern mountains of Haiti. We planned to visit several orphanages, schools, and churches that were part of the nonprofit my late husband and I started years ago.

One of my local friends came to visit us at the guest house where we were staying. She brought her baby, who was only a few weeks old. My girls and I were enthralled with this sweet little one. Her delicate eyelashes, her milk-chocolate skin, and the curve of her cheeks were almost too much. She was like a doll.

We took turns holding her and cooing over her while she slept on that hot Haitian afternoon. My youngest daughter, Zayla, asked if she could have a turn holding her. I hesitated, but saw the earnest look in her eyes. The baby's mama nodded in agreement, and I gently laid the baby in Zayla's arms.

The two sat blissfully on the hand-carved wooden bench in the entrance of our guest house. My own baby girl—now seven years old—held this new baby with such tender care.

"Mama, why is she wrapped in a towel?" Zayla asked.

"I don't think she has a blanket," I said softly.

Zayla locked eyes with me. "She needs a blanket," she said decisively. She rose and passed the baby back into my arms.

My husband Shawn and I looked at each other. I know we both had the same thought: *Would our girl surrender her beloved blanket?* We'd had many conversations about entitlement and compassion with this child in particular. Was God moving her heart?

Zayla came bounding down the tile steps holding her treasured blanket—the super-soft, rainbow-colored, furry fleece one. The blanket that we had to find each night before bed and that we'd chased through airports to retrieve. We were all awed by this spontaneous expression of generosity.

That night as I was tucking Zayla into bed, she whispered, "Mama, I miss my blanket."

"I know you do, honey," I replied.

"But I'm still glad I gave it to that baby," she said.

My mama heart simply smiled. She was leading us all.

—DORINA LAZO GILMORE-YOUNG

When have you been moved with compassion to give up something that was precious to you? Or when has someone done this for you?

As we finish out our fourth week of this study, we're going to dive straight into Scripture, because what we're about to hear from Peter is just too good to delay. Lean in.

He writes, "Above all, love each other deeply, because love covers over a multitude of sins. Offer hospitality to one another without grumbling. Each of you should use whatever gift you have received to serve others, as faithful stewards of God's grace in its various forms" (1 Peter 4:8–10 NIV).

Above all. Don't those words just perk up your ears and settle your soul? It's like a little blinking neon sign signaling our heart and mind to pay attention. Sometimes it all can feel too much, right? The noise of the world, the demands of the day, maybe even being a Christian or reading the Bible—all of it can feel overwhelming. That's okay. *Above all* means we can temporarily let go of everything else and simply remember what's most important.

So what's the thing that matters above all? *Love others deeply.* Of course.

What does Peter say love does? How has this been true in your life?

What does it look like to "offer hospitality to one another without grumbling"? How does this require courageous kindness?

Several translations of 1 Peter 4:10 include the phrase "manifold grace of God." One commentary explains that Peter uses "grace" not in its theological sense but "in the sense of bountiful giving; and the beautiful word rendered 'manifold' brings out the subtle and picturesque variety with which God arranges and distributes His bounty. But the emphatic word of the sentence is 'of God.'"[3]

Do you see what the commentator is saying? Peter isn't just talking about God's grace that saves us from eternal separation from Him (i.e., death). Peter is talking about *all* that God has given us that leads to abundant *life*!

> **As God's daughters and co-heirs with Christ, we get to receive the riches of Yahweh's love, kindness, goodness, and faithfulness.**

As God's daughters and co-heirs with Christ, we get to receive the riches of Yahweh's love, kindness, goodness, and faithfulness. That is the grace of God. And then we have the privilege—the high calling—of sharing that bounty of God's grace with others in return.

Showing deep love and hospitality by using the gift you've been given to steward the manifold grace of God sometimes means stretching a few ingredients and adding another seat at the table. Other times it means showing up with a pickup truck to help a friend move, or listening to a child after a long tiresome day. And sometimes it means giving up a beloved blanket.

Read Peter's continuing instructions in 1 Peter 4:11. Whose strength are we to rely on to carry out these things, and who gets the praise and glory? How does bringing the focus back to God take the pressure off or give you freedom in loving and serving others?

_____

_____

_____

_____

Read 2 Corinthians 1:3–5 in the New International Version. What reason is given for why God comforts us? What comes after the *so that*?

_____

_____

_____

_____

_____

Even as a young child, Zayla understood what it means to comfort others with the comfort she herself has received. Zayla knows what it's like to be cold, to feel scared or unsure, and she knows the gift of being wrapped in a bright and cozy blanket. She understands how that physical comfort also brings comfort to a little girl's heart. Zayla was moved with compassion for another—a compassion that helped her choose personal sacrifice and inconvenience.

God lavishly offers us compassion because that's who He is and He loves us. But God's compassion doesn't stop there. He calls each of us to "pay it forward" at home with our families, on the job with our co-workers, or on a trip to another country. Whether it's with your neighbor, a grocery store worker, or a stranger on the street corner, God is inviting you to give what He's given you. Show compassion even when it's inconvenient. Love well so that people will know you belong to Jesus, and God will get the praise.

At the tender age of seven, Zayla is becoming a woman of courageous kindness. Surely we can follow her example.

Think back. In what ways has "the Father of compassion and the God of all comfort" comforted you? Be specific. How might He want to use the experience of your past afflictions to comfort someone in their present situation?

_____

_____

_____

_____

_____

Reflect on this prayer and make it your own today:

Father, thank You for giving me Your Word and making it clear what's most important. You have loved me—poured out Your compassion and grace on me—and I want to do the same for others. Help me to hold loosely to my own comfort and worldly possessions so that I'm ready to give them up for the sake of another. All I have is Yours. Lead me in a life of courageous kindness this week. Amen.

> ▶ For a deeper look at this week's study and to spur on discussion if you're working with a small group, watch a FREE video from (in)courage at incourage.me/biblestudy.

for the long haul

But when he saw the strength of the wind, he was afraid, and beginning to sink he cried out, "LORD, save me!" Immediately Jesus reached out his hand, [and] caught hold of him.

Matthew 14:30–31

She stopped me in the foyer after church and asked if we could meet for coffee sometime. Her voice didn't betray urgency, but her eyes told me she had things to get off her chest. I told her to come over for dinner during the week so that we could have the leisure of time to chat after I put the kids to bed. We scheduled an evening, and I couldn't help feeling curious about what would come of our time together.

As I prepped for dinner, I prayed for wisdom to hear this woman's heart and for insight to share if she asked me to. I put together a meal of comfort—seaweed soup and side dishes to go along with rice, just like my mother used to make—and some brownies to top dinner off on a sweet note.

When she arrived, we seamlessly flowed into conversation even though we hadn't known each other for very long. She had only recently started coming to our church, and other than our brief interactions during the "introduce yourself to a neighbor" time during the service, we weren't well acquainted.

By dessert, she was ready to share her story of pain and addiction and not knowing how to deal with the anger and shame. She'd held the words for so long in the dark that as they tumbled out into the light, she hardly made sense.

We wept together as she shared about the abuse she had endured by those who were supposed to be safe and loving. She apologized for her tears, for laying so much on me, but I gently reminded her that tears are necessary for healing and that I was there to carry the pain with her.

That dinner was the first of many. We walked together as she sought counsel from professionals who could help with her addictions. We discussed how to create boundaries where needed, and as much as I could, I tried to show her how beloved she was by God. Mostly, we spent time together—running errands to Target, taking strolls in the evenings with my family, and of course, eating.

Over the years, I got to witness God's miraculous grace as this woman slowly began to heal. Through every victory, every setback, and every comeback, His kindness was present through the help of friends and community, therapists and healthy relationships. And with my own eyes, I got to see the persistent love God has for us and how His joy becomes ours when we walk the long haul with others.

—GRACE P. CHO

How does walking with someone for an extended season help you see more of God?

Friend! We've made it to week 5 in our study, and we still have so much to discover about God's character and His plan for us to live as women made for courageous kindness.

This week is all about the long haul. Sometimes we're tempted to put kindness in a box labeled "random acts" or "one and done." But often courageous kindness looks like investing in relationships over time. It looks like showing up again and again for someone. Being present, loving, caring, generous, and forgiving—when it's easy *and* when it's hard.

As we've seen throughout the course of this study, God's kindness in our lives is perpetual, continual. What a relief that God is not easily deterred by our doubts or complaints or wayward ways. His love pursues us even when we're like stubborn kids with selective hearing who think we know better than our Father.

> **God's kindness in our lives is perpetual, continual.**

Need evidence that this is true? Just think of Peter.

Oh, Peter. God bless him.

Last week we studied Peter's teaching about using our gifts to serve others and being good stewards of God's grace. But Peter wasn't always so wise. Scripture's first accounts of Peter—one of the twelve disciples and part of Jesus's inner circle—show a different side. He was passionate and impulsive. He reacted before he stopped to consider the consequences. He interrupted and contradicted Jesus. He trusted Jesus and then let fear overtake him. Peter swore his loyalty to Jesus and then denied Him three times.

Suffice it to say, Peter wasn't a perfect friend. And yet Jesus loved him relentlessly. Jesus showed up on the shore and in the storm. He predicted Peter's duplicity and still welcomed him with open arms.

Read Matthew 14:22–32. (Note: this story takes place right after the feeding of the five thousand.) What was the first thing Jesus said to the disciples? What was the first thing Jesus did when Peter cried out for help?

What do Jesus's responses tell you about Him and how He engages with those He loves?

"You of little faith, why did you doubt?"

Was Jesus's question laced with frustration? Was it an accusation? Scripture doesn't specify His tone, but from what we know of God's character, chances are good that Jesus's reply to scared and sinking Peter was fueled by compassion, not condemnation. Read His words with the inflection of a concerned friend. The voice of a kind parent who longs to see their child grow in maturity and trust.

Peter, along with the other disciples, had just witnessed Jesus multiply a few small loaves of bread and a couple fish into a satisfying feast for thousands. And yet Peter forgets the evidence of God's provision. He doubts Jesus's power. Still Jesus reaches out.

Jesus sees us in our weakness and in our doubt, but rather than wagging a "can't you just get it together" finger, He grabs hold of us, gripping us with His comfort and assurance. Despite Peter's wavering faith, Jesus didn't let him sink. When our life storms come, surely He will meet us there too.

Read Psalm 107:28–31 and Luke 8:22–25. What did God/Jesus do for those in the storm? When has He met you in a stormy season or situation?

_____

_____

_____

_____

Since Jesus no longer walks this earth, He often asks us to be His hands and feet to others. How can you courageously offer a calm word or the support of your presence to someone in a storm this week?

_____

_____

_____

_____

Perhaps the greatest example of Jesus's long-haul kindness in Peter's life had less to do with being there in physical storms and more to do with guiding Peter through his emotional and spiritual storms.

In Matthew 16, Peter is the first disciple to proclaim the truth of Jesus's true identity: "You are the Messiah, the Son of the living God" (v. 16). But as soon as Jesus explains that this means He must suffer and ultimately be killed, Peter has the audacity to rebuke Him: "Oh no, Lord! This will never happen to you!" (v. 22). Later, when Jesus washes the disciples' feet before the Passover feast as an example of what it means to serve one another, Peter doesn't understand and refuses to let his Lord perform such a lowly task for him (John 13:8). Yet after Jesus explains that this is the way to be part of what He is doing, Peter changes his tune to the opposite extreme and asks Jesus to wash not only his feet but his hands and head too (v. 9).

And then of course it's recorded in all four Gospels how, on the very night that Jesus is arrested and tried, Peter denies his Lord three times.

And Jesus keeps loving him.

It takes courage to be in relationship with others, doesn't it? It takes courage to make space for someone else's sin and pain, for their messy emotions and tangled words. But like Grace expressed in our opening story, we also find so much hope and beauty when we're willing to open our heart to someone for the long haul. We don't have to come with all the answers. We're not meant to be anyone's savior. We're simply meant to say with our everyday lives, *I see you. I'm committed to walking with you. Let's seek God together in the middle of our mess.*

Look up Matthew 8:14–15; 17:1–4; and 18:21–22. What do these additional snapshots tell you about Jesus and Peter's relationship?

How does today's study encourage your heart to invest in someone for the long haul? Who is God asking you to show His kindness to today?

Reflect on this prayer and make it your own today:

Jesus, thank You for loving me when my faith is strong and when it sinks. Thank You for pursuing me when I'm following hard after You and when I'm wrapped up in my own misguided thinking. Help me to remember all the ways You've been kind to me so that I may have the patience and tenacity to be there for others. Amen.

Now Jesus loved Martha, her sister, and Lazarus.

John 11:5

When my friend made the offer, I didn't even know what to say. I mean, of course the answer was an emphatic yes! But I was also speechless.

My boys were five, four, and two that summer when my friend Mindy asked if she could watch them for a couple hours one day a week to give me time to write—or do whatever I needed, or just be. As a mom with littles, time alone was the most scarce and sacred resource. I longed for it, prayed for it. Mindy knew this from experience because she had two girls around the same ages as my sons.

What boggled my mind and made a lasting imprint on my heart and in our friendship was the fact that Mindy wasn't just helping me in a pinch or stepping in during a crisis. She was actively looking for a way to love me, to invest in our friendship by serving me on an ongoing basis. And the kicker? She did so without asking for anything in return.

I remember one particular morning that summer when I spent two glorious hours at Corner Bakery savoring a caramel latte and a large piece of cinnamon coffee cake while working on a blog post for my tiny corner of the internet. I was so full of gratitude for this slice of time away. Yet as soon as I pulled back into Mindy's driveway, I broke down in unexpected and uncontrollable tears.

What's wrong with me? I cried out to God as my friend helped buckle my squirmy, didn't-want-to-leave boys into their car seats. I felt ashamed of the emotions I couldn't name or explain. *Was I not thankful enough? Did I not love my kids and my life enough? Did I not trust God enough with the things that weighed heavy on my heart even after enjoying the gift of my friend's kindness?*

But Mindy didn't judge my tears. She just hugged me. She reminded me that I'm a great mom and it's okay to cry even if you don't know why. She told me that my boys were wonderful and she loved having them over.

"I can't wait until next week!" she said, standing with her sweet daughters in the driveway and waving us goodbye.

—BECKY KEIFE

Has a friend ever gifted you time or service over the long haul? What did it mean to you?

_____

_____

_____

_____

One of the most remarkable things about Jesus is that He chose to make close friends and invest His life in them. God's Son—who is fully divine and who became fully human to accomplish the will of the Father—chose to spend His short earthly years being a really good friend to some really messy people. Isn't that the best?

Sure, many people had but a single, brief encounter with the Messiah. The woman who reached through the crowd and touched the hem of His garment. The paralyzed man who was lowered through the roof by his friends. The blind man who received sight through dirt mixed with spit and Jesus's miracle touch. Yes, Jesus can make a life-changing impact through a single moment or meeting.

But think about the disciples and the inner circle of friends Jesus shared life with. The ones He showed up for time and time again. The ones He saw at their worst and loved them anyway. The continual kindness of their friend Jesus made all the difference.

The ripple of His influence in their lives created waves of lasting change.

Look up Matthew 9:10; Luke 9:18; and Luke 22:39. What do these small examples tell you about how Jesus did life with His disciples?

_____

_____

_____

_____

The Gospels show that, in addition to the disciples, Jesus had several other close friends, including two sisters named Mary and Martha. Read Scripture's first mention of them in Luke 10:38–42. What does Martha's tone imply about her relationship with Jesus?

_____

_____

_____

_____

Clearly, Martha can't handle the seeming inequity between her frantic preparations and Mary's lounging at the feet of Jesus, and she doesn't keep quiet about it. "Lord, don't you care that my sister has left me to serve alone? So tell her to give me a hand" (Luke 10:40). Doesn't that sound like the voice of a friend who is close enough to be like a sister?

for the long haul

Martha calls Him Lord out of respect, but her words reveal Jesus wasn't an unfamiliar guest. If this had been the first time they met, surely Martha would have maintained a more formal tone, shown more restraint, and stifled the exasperation she felt toward her unhelpful sister.

But good friends don't need to filter their feelings. They say it like it is. And that's exactly what busy, distracted, irritated Martha did.

Jesus's response confirms the nature of their friendship. "Martha, Martha," he responds, affectionately repeating her name. He knows her. He knows how she gets tightly wound and loses sight of what's truly important. He probably also knows their family dynamics and any underlying tension between the sisters. Jesus doesn't rebuke Martha's brutal honesty like an elite leader casting judgment.

He responds like a friend—calling her out and up and loving her right where she is.

Let's look at another encounter when Martha is grieving something far more serious than unevenly divided chores. Read John 11:1–7. How do the sisters identify their brother? What does verse 5 say about how Jesus felt toward these three siblings?

Continue reading verses 17–37. What does Jesus promise Martha (v. 23)? Even knowing this, how does Jesus respond to His friends' grief (vv. 32–35)?

Jesus came to Bethany to help His friends, but He also entered into their sorrow. Jesus had already told the disciples and Martha that Lazarus would be raised from the dead. Nevertheless, He chose to share in their suffering.

Consider how Jesus could have responded. He could have patted Mary on the head and told her that her tears were for nothing because He was about to bring Lazarus back to life. He could have scolded her for not trusting Him more. He could have given a "just wait and see" sermon about the power of God. But this moment wasn't so much about what Jesus was going to do; it was about being present with His friends.

If we can experience the comfort of a friend opening her arms to us and sharing our tears—whether in times of crisis or just on the long hard road of singleness or chronic illness or fill-in-the-blank ordinary life—then just imagine the deep love and comfort Mary and Martha felt when Jesus wept alongside them.

This is the kindness of Christ.

You can read the rest of the story in John 11:38–44, but here's a spoiler: Jesus makes good on His word. Lazarus comes back to life!

> **The kindness of a long-haul friend is the kindness of God.**

Revel in this miracle, and then camp out on this thought: Jesus went to extraordinary lengths in meeting Mary and Martha in their grief and raising Lazarus from the dead because *He knew them* and He loved them.

The kindness of a long-haul friend is the kindness of God. This is who Jesus is and who He invites us to be.

How does Jesus's example inspire you to be a long-haul friend? Record any additional insights or key verses you want to remember.

_____

_____

_____

_____

How can you courageously and intentionally invest in a friendship or serve someone today?

_____

_____

_____

_____

Reflect on this prayer and make it your own today:

Oh Jesus, what a friend I have in You. Thank You for reminding me of Your love and loyalty through the pages of Scripture and the stories in my own life. Help me to follow Your example of loving others well. Empower me today to live a life of courageous kindness for the long haul. Amen.

We cared so much for you that we were pleased to
share with you not only the gospel of God but also our
own lives, because you had become dear to us.

1 Thessalonians 2:8

One of the greatest life and faith lessons I've learned
is that there's no such thing as *unanswered* prayer.
This isn't always easy to accept (or even believe), especially when it seems like God is silent. But I've seen in
my own life that sometimes His love and kindness are
expressed when we *don't* get what we want (or think we
want).

Many years ago, when our family moved to a new state, we left behind a large circle of friends. I knew finding our people was crucial—as
individuals, a couple, and a family. I was thankful my children quickly
made friends at their new school, but friendships were slower to de-
velop for my husband and me. Though becoming active members of
various church groups provided us automatic connection and relationship, depth was missing. I begged God to bring kindred friendships into
our lives, but community hovered on the surface.

My relational voids allowed more time for me to invest in my
children and their friends as they navigated the complexities of high
school. This wasn't helicopter parenting, but my being available and
present made space for the hard conversations these teenagers wanted
and needed to have with a trusted adult. Learning how to listen without
reacting or judging kept them talking.

My children are now young adults, and their friends continue to stay in touch. I grinned like crazy when my son's best friend from high school texted me for one of my recipes. *Really . . . glazed carrots?* My heart exploded when my daughter's BFF wrote to thank me for teaching her hospitality by simply being hospitable and always making time for her.

The types of friendship and community I envisioned for myself may not have materialized when my children were in high school, but I realize how kind and gracious God was to give me a community that needed me during that season. Had my prayers been answered according to *my* ideal, I would have missed out on something special and precious.

We may not *feel* God's kindness when we don't get what we want, but that doesn't mean He isn't being kind. Give it a little time, look in the rearview mirror, and tell me what you see.

—ROBIN DANCE

Have you ever longed for a friendship or community that looked a certain way? How did (or could) your willingness to invest in the people in front of you make a difference?

As we continue to examine what courageous kindness looks like from a long-haul perspective, today's study takes us to the life of Paul and his friendship with a young man named Timothy.

Timothy is first introduced in Acts 16 when Paul visited Lystra and chose him as a ministry partner and traveling companion. In the very first verse we learn two important things about Timothy: his mother was a believing Jew and his father was a Greek (i.e., Gentile). Acts 16:3 says that Timothy was uncircumcised, which meant that He would not have been allowed to enter the temple—the most prominent place of Jewish teaching, worship, and community.

Okay, so you might be wondering, *Why in the world is this important, and what does it have to do with becoming women of courageous kindness?* Hang on. We'll get there.

So that's the CliffsNotes version of Timothy's history. Now let's look at Paul.

In Acts 9:1–22, Paul transforms from a persecutor of Christians to a Christian preacher. How do you think Paul's conversion helped him continue to surrender his plans and expectations to God?

Read Philippians 3:3–6 to learn more about Paul's background. Based on this, what do you think Paul would have originally expected or hoped for in a young disciple?

Paul's and Timothy's diverse backgrounds emphasize the fact that we don't have to come from the same place or have been raised in the same traditions to build a meaningful relationship. Paul, the former Christian-killer, took Timothy, the half-Jewish kid who had no prestigious religious training, under his spiritual wing—all because of Jesus. Timothy was likely just a teenager when Paul came into his life. Over the course of nearly twenty years, Timothy would travel side by side with Paul, learning about the things of Christ and passing them on to others.

> **We don't have to come from the same place or have been raised in the same traditions to build a meaningful relationship.**

In his first letter to the church at Thessalonica, Paul, together with Timothy and Silas, reflects on their previous visit:

> Even though we had some standing as Christ's apostles, we never threw our weight around or tried to come across as important, with you or anyone else. We weren't aloof with you. We took you just as you were. We were never patronizing, never condescending, but we cared for you the way a mother cares for her children. We loved you dearly. Not content to just pass on the Message, we wanted to give you our hearts. And we *did*. (1 Thess. 2:6–8 MSG)

Paul invested in Timothy over the long haul, modeling for other believers what it looks like to love, care for, and come alongside one another.

Keep reading in 1 Thessalonians 2:9–12. What metaphor does Paul use for their relationship with the believers? What does this tell you about your opportunity to help, train, and nurture others regardless of age or shared DNA?

The Message paraphrases verses 11–12 like this: "With each of you we were like a father with his child, holding your hand, whispering encouragement, showing you step-by-step how to live well before God, who called us into his own kingdom, into this delightful life." If someone has showed you this sort of kindness, what did it look like and what impact did it make? Who in your life could you do this for?

Over time, Paul and Timothy grew from mentor and mentee into a father-son duo who were true partners in the gospel (Phil. 2:19–22). Imagine the countless conversations they had on dusty roads and in storm-tossed boats, the meals they shared in new and familiar places, and the desperate prayers they prayed together in the face of suffering and persecution. Surely it wasn't always easy. Like in any relationship, they must've had plenty of awkward, irritating, and frustrating moments. But what's clear is that these two guys from different generations and different upbringings were committed to each other and to growing in Christ together.

Paul's ministry ended with a final letter to Timothy. Even while he was in prison, Paul continued to invest in the spiritual development of his friend. He wanted to pass on every bit of wisdom, every hard-earned lesson to encourage and strengthen the man who had become like a son to him.

The world will tell you to find friendships that are easy and make you feel good. It says to look for a community that will serve you well and meet your needs. But God says, *Look out for the interests of others before your own.* God says, *I made you for community, and I'll lead you in cultivating it.*

Like Paul in the New Testament and Robin in our opening story, we have the opportunity (and responsibility) to look for ways to invest in others. Maybe there's a younger mom at your church or a new co-worker in the corner cubicle whom you could encourage. Maybe it's the teenager down the street or your own kid in the next room who needs the love and counsel only you can give.

Paul didn't just let Timothy watch him preach a handful of times. Robin wasn't available just once for the teens who flooded her kitchen after school. Their investment was over the long haul. They offered the kindness of their presence, the kindness of their very lives. And surely they experienced the kindness of God through all they received in return.

Read 2 Timothy 1:1–5. What stands out to you? Besides Paul, who else made an impact in Timothy's life?

How does today's study encourage you to invest in an unlikely friendship or pour your life into someone a few steps behind you in life or faith?

Reflect on this prayer and make it your own today:

God, thank You for creating me for community. I know sometimes I can cling to my own ideas of what that should look like or what it means. Help me today to open my eyes and heart to whomever You want me to do life with. Any little bit You've given me, I want to share with others. Show me who. Show me how. I'm expectant for what only You can do. Amen.

God had granted Daniel kindness and compassion from
the chief eunuch.

Daniel 1:9

I rolled out of bed bleary-eyed and heavy-hearted most mornings. As a newly minted widow and suddenly single mama of three, exhaustion was the norm for me. My girls were two, five, and eight, and their needs were great. Not to mention my work and the household chores I now had to cover on my own. But I knew if I didn't take this early-morning time that I might not have another moment to myself for the rest of the day. So each morning I would brush my teeth, grab my Bible and journal, tiptoe out to our big red couch in the front room, and hope no little girls would hear me.

The couch faced a big picture window. I pulled back the chocolate-colored curtains. The Japanese maple tree outside waved to me each morning with its warm jewel-toned leaves. I snuggled under my bulky knit blanket in the glow of the lamp.

This was the only quiet time when I could meet with my heavenly Father.

My late husband, Ericlee, used to take each of our three girls on daddy dates. He wanted to spend one-on-one time with them, so they would go out for ice cream, play at the park, or take a bike ride. It was their special time together.

In those wee morning hours, I had my daddy date with God.

I shared my struggles with Him in prayer as if we were on a coffee date. I pored over Scripture—reading about Ruth and Job, clinging to David's prayers of lament, and looking for answers to my questions about heaven. I scribbled in my gratitude journal, recording the ways I saw God at work even in the darkness.

As I navigated grief, loneliness, and uncertainty about the future, God sat with me there. His presence was palpable. On the red couch, God met me morning after morning. Now I can look back on that season—which stretched like a too-tight sweater over months and years—and see His steadfast kindness toward me.

Some miracles happen in a moment; some happen over the long haul. I believe God performed a miracle in me over time, healing my heart one daddy date at a time.

—DORINA LAZO GILMORE-YOUNG

What's one way you've experienced the steadfast kindness of God? (We've talked about this a lot, but keep digging deep and training your eyes to see His kindness-wrapped love in your life!)

Yesterday we saw how Paul experienced a dramatic conversion when Jesus met him on the road to Damascus and changed everything (Acts 9). Back in week 2 we saw how in a single meeting with Jesus, Zacchaeus went from being a greedy tax collector to a man willing to give away half of his possessions to the poor and pay back the people he had cheated fourfold.

God is powerful enough to make radical changes in our lives in an instant. But as Dorina shared, God's miracles of transformation often happen over the long haul—one moment, one small kindness at a time. Today we're going to see how this played out in the life of Daniel.

> **God's miracles of transformation often happen over the long haul—one moment, one small kindness at a time.**

When we think of Daniel, often the first thing that comes to mind is a harrowing picture of him being thrown into the lions' den. No doubt the angels sent to close their devouring jaws was the kindness of God! But this was just one of many moments when God's kindness and presence made a difference in Daniel's life.

Read Daniel 1:1–16. How is God's kindness and compassion displayed to Daniel? What was the ultimate outcome?

Continue reading verses 17–21. How is God's favor displayed in the lives of Daniel and the three other young men? How do you think Daniel's conviction to follow God's ways even in a foreign land played a role?

Daniel was an Israelite from the tribe of Judah who had been taken captive during the Babylonian siege of Jerusalem. He was an exile, a foreigner at the mercy of a king and culture that did not know or respect Yahweh. Yet Daniel didn't waver in his personal commitment to God. And God didn't waver in His kindness to Daniel.

In chapter 2 we read the story of King Nebuchadnezzar's troubling dream. The king demanded that his magicians, sorcerers, and astrologers tell him the specific details of his dream and then interpret it. When they were unable to fulfill his impossible request, the enraged king ordered all the wise men in Babylon to be executed. Daniel and his friends were some of the wise men, so the king's guard came for them too.

Read Daniel 2:14–24. How does Daniel's response to the captain of the guard and to the king reflect what was stated back in Daniel 1:17?

What three things did Daniel do after he asked the king for more time to interpret the dream?

When his career was on the line and his very life was at stake, Daniel gathered with his friends. The men had been together from their capture as teenagers through their three years of training in the king's palace. Clearly Daniel knew that it was God who could answer his prayers for divine revelation and deliverance. Yet Daniel's actions also show that he knew the value of linking arms with friends who are in it with you for the long haul.

The balance of chapter 2 reveals that indeed God answered Daniel's prayer and allowed him to accurately describe and interpret the king's dream. In response, Nebuchadnezzar fell down and worshiped God. He also promoted Daniel, gave him gifts, and honored Daniel's request to let his friends manage the province of Babylon.

The kindness of God doesn't always equate to material wealth or prestigious positions of influence. Sometimes His kindness is the nourishment that comes from vegetables. Sometimes it's the unexpected compassion from someone in authority. Sometimes His kindness is in a cozy blanket, the leaves of a maple tree, and His continual presence through life's hardest moments.

If you have time today or in the future, continue reading through the book of Daniel and record all the moments where the steadfast kindness of God was evident in his life.

Now think about your own life. Look back over the years or just the past week. In what ways big and small has God showed that He was with you then, is with you now, and will be with you for the long haul?

Reflect on this prayer and make it your own today:

God, You are powerful and faithful and good—not just occasionally but relentlessly. I see that through the pages of Scripture and through my own life. Keep opening my eyes to the evidence of Your kindness so that I might give You all the praise You deserve. Put Your presence on display in my life, Lord, so that others may come to know You too. Amen.

By yourself you're unprotected.
With a friend you can face the worst.
Can you round up a third?
A three-stranded rope isn't easily snapped.
Ecclesiastes 4:12 MSG

When two of my friends and I formed a book club years ago, we had no idea what we were getting into. It was just the three of us, each woman feeling like she wasn't reading enough. We thought an accountability system ought to do the trick. But Book Club quickly became about more than just reading books.

I looked forward to those once-a-week meetups. I knew I would leave refreshed and thankful and filled with coffee. Most of the time the books remained untouched. Instead, we talked. The three of us often took turns weeping over the sorrow we were facing: divorce, death, sexual abuse. Each of our lives connected at the time when we needed it most. I knew then just as I know now, Book Club had the kindness of God written all over it.

When my friend was in the midst of her divorce, the three of us held one another on her couch, each of us clinging to the woman next to her. The three of us were smooshed together so tight you couldn't even tell whose arms belonged to who. We cried and prayed and clung to one another for hours. We also spent three days at the beach to get away from the reality that felt crushing to her. We ate a lot of cheese and ice cream.

When my other friend got pregnant and was terrified, we rallied around her. We didn't ask questions she wasn't ready to answer. When she had her stunningly beautiful baby, we were there in the weeks afterward, eager to celebrate and support.

When I was ready to face what I'd been through with my ex-boyfriend, a sexual assault I had never wanted to talk about, it was my Book Club friends who walked alongside me. They cried. They told me it was real. They drove me to therapy.

In that same year, all three of us ended up going to the same counseling center. There were so many times during Book Club when we'd find ourselves discussing counseling only to burst out laughing. Our lives felt like such messes—and yet by the grace of God, we had each other.

We've only completed one book since we started Book Club so many years ago, but perhaps forming an actual book club was never the point. Maybe the point all along, whether we knew it or not, was friendship. And this friendship will stick with me forever.

—ALIZA LATTA

Have you ever experienced the gift of an unexpected friendship? Describe what that friendship meant to you.

_____

_____

_____

_____

The kindness of God is demonstrated through relationship. This is a drum I'll beat as loud and often as needed because it's so vitally important to how we view God and how we view our purpose on this planet.

The triune God exists in relationship with Himself. Jesus came to earth to be in relationship with people and walk with them for thirty-three dusty years. His life, death, and resurrection were all for the ultimate purpose of restoring humanity into right relationship with our Creator to the glory of God.

This is why we are not meant to live as silos. We are not individuals who are meant to exist in protective bubbles that save us from being bumped and bruised by other humans. Rather, we are individuals who form different parts of one interconnected body. The evidence is clear: Moses needed Aaron and Hur to hold up his arms while Joshua fought the battle. The hungry crowd was fed when the boy gave what he had to help feed his community. The paralyzed man needed the literal arms and legs of his friends. Jesus was connected to the hearts of Mary, Martha, and Lazarus. Peter was passionately tethered to His Savior.

So we also are meant to do life together.

> **We are individuals who form different parts of one interconnected body.**

Read Ecclesiastes 4:9–12. What's the main idea and takeaway?

How have you experienced this to be true in your own life?

Consider how The Message paraphrases these verses: "By yourself you're unprotected. With a friend you can face the worst. Can you round up a third? A three-stranded rope isn't easily snapped." Notice how there is an underlying assumption that at some point we *will* face the worst. We will need to be protected, lifted up, kept warm.

We hear this echo of warning and hope reverberate through the ages, from the Old Testament to the New. Around nine hundred years after Ecclesiastes was written, Jesus told His disciples, "In this world you will have trouble. But take heart! I have overcome the world" (John 16:33 NIV).

In each of these passages, we see a contrast between life alone and life together. As we know, hardship, suffering, and sorrow are part of this world. But God provides continual counsel and companionship through the Holy Spirit. Plus, no matter what battles we face today, Christ has conquered death and secured our forever home in heaven.

As we've looked at earlier this week and throughout the study, God doesn't stop at our eternal salvation. He also cares deeply about our day-to-day lives. God is with us for the long haul *and* He designed us to be there for one another. It's why Jesus wept over the death of Lazarus even though He knew His friend would live again. It's why Jesus asked Peter, James, and John to come to the garden and pray with Him on the eve of His crucifixion. It's why Paul loved Timothy and did ministry together with him.

We need each other.

Read Ruth 1. What did Naomi expect her daughters-in-law to do after their husbands died? What did Ruth choose to do instead?

What does this tell you about what Ruth and Naomi's relationship must have been like *before* adversity hit?

In kindness, Naomi wanted what was best for these two women she had grown to love as daughters. Naomi knew she couldn't provide for her daughters-in-law, so she insisted they part ways—Orpah and Ruth going back to their families of origin, and Naomi returning to her home country of Judah that she had left a decade earlier.

But Ruth was less concerned about the security of her own future and wholly focused on loving and supporting her mother-in-law in her time of greatest need. Certainly, it would have been easier for Ruth to bail. To return to her own family and grieve her husband's death and look for a more hopeful future. No one would have blamed her. Yet Ruth was resolute in sticking with Naomi through the hard. She knew two were better than one. When everything was stripped away, Ruth kept loving.

In today's opening story, we see the beauty of a similar outpouring of friendship between Aliza and her book club friends. In the midst of intense personal trials, each woman experienced the kindness of God through the kindness of her friends.

Surely Jesus would love to sit on a couch next to us and wrap His arms around us as we weep. But for such a time as this, we get to be His arms for one another.

Read 1 Corinthians 12:25–26 in your favorite translation. Then look it up in The Message using your Bible app or at BibleGateway.com. How does it describe God's design for the body of Christ?

How might God be asking you to sit (or walk or drive) with a friend who is suffering? How can you show them the kindness of Jesus in their time of trouble?

Reflect on this prayer and make it your own today:

Jesus, thank You for conquering the world and for caring deeply about my daily life. I recognize that You designed me for community—in good times and in bad. Open the door to new friendships. Give me courage to love others well for the long haul. Thank You for being with me in it. Amen.

> ▶ For a deeper look at this week's study and to spur on discussion if you're working with a small group, watch a FREE video from (in)courage at incourage.me/biblestudy.

more than you expected

> The flour jar did not become empty, and the oil jug did not run dry, according to the word of the LORD he had spoken through Elijah.
>
> 1 Kings 17:16

When my son Elias was born, my joy doubled—and so did my overwhelm. Early mornings blurred into long afternoons that stretched into sleepless nights. Having babies nineteen months apart was never the plan. I cried constantly out of both gratitude and exhaustion.

I felt so alone. I ached to see God. To know He hadn't abandoned me in the land of spit-up and Cheerios. Consumed by life with a newborn and a tiny toddler, I wondered if I could still make a difference beyond my four walls.

The answer came in a way I had never expected—through breast milk.

My baby nursed around the clock, yet my breasts were engorged. I pumped extra milk to bring physical relief and with the hope that Elias would learn to take a bottle.

Day after day, week after week, he refused the bottle and my body refused to stop producing excess milk. I read books that said to simply stop pumping and eventually the supply would decrease. While this was sound advice, I felt compelled to keep pumping. My firstborn had taken a bottle like a champ, and an ample supply of frozen breast milk gave me the flexibility for an occasional night out. I was holding on to hope that my efforts to store up extra milk would pay off.

One morning I was out walking with a friend whose daughter had been born just a couple weeks after Elias. We pushed our strollers side by side, panting up the steep tree-lined street and exchanging motherhood stories. As we neared the top of the hill, my friend shared that she was having trouble feeding her baby. Not just that the baby wouldn't latch correctly, but that she wasn't producing enough milk, and every formula they tried upset her daughter's tummy.

"I'm trying to increase my production by pumping, but after thirty minutes I barely have half an ounce to show for it," she said, frustration and heartache in every syllable.

The picture of my freezer overflowing with bags of breast milk flashed in my mind. At first I felt guilty. Then I had an idea. My heart pounded in my chest—less because of the strain of pushing a double stroller and more because I was nervous. Questions swirled in my mind. *What if I offend her? What if it gets awkward? What if I regret it?*

Finally, I said, "Hey . . . I don't know how you would feel about this, but I have a freezer full of breast milk, and Elias won't take a bottle. If you want the milk, it's yours."

"Really?" she replied.

Later that night my friend arrived with an ice chest. Together we filled it with liquid gold, barely holding back tears. From a place of lack, God brought abundance. We both stood in awe, undone by His kindness.

—BECKY KEIFE

Have you ever doubted your ability to make a difference? How have you seen God work in your life in an expected yet providential way?

As we conclude this exploration of how our small, ordinary, courageous acts of intentional kindness can make an impact in the world, there's something we need to make sure we've heard loud and clear: *it's not about us.*

The goal was not to get to the end of this study with a resolve to simply do more and try harder. If you're focused on hustling enough to be kind enough, you've missed the point. Does living the simple difference take action and intention on our part? Absolutely. But it also takes a surrendered heart. Which leads to two primary questions for you to chew on this week:

1. What if the display of God's power in your life is directly related to acknowledging your need for Him?
2. What if you can't be part of creating a tidal wave of positive change until you positively grasp how much you need God?

Keep those questions in your mind as we turn to 1 Kings 17 and read the story of a woman who was certain she had nothing left to give that could make a difference.

Read 1 Kings 17:8–16. How would you describe the woman's circumstances and state of mind? What do you think compelled her to do what Elijah asked even though logically it didn't make sense?

What ultimately happened? What does verse 16 attribute the outcome to?

Have you ever felt at the end of your rope, like all hope was lost? Like if God didn't intervene ASAP, you weren't going to make it? No doubt that's how the widow felt. She was ready to fix a final meal for herself and her son and then just give up.

But what does Elijah say to her after hearing about her dire situation? "Don't be afraid" (v. 13). Elijah's words to the widow are the same words God spoke to Joshua before he crossed into the promised land: *Do not be afraid.* (Remember how we looked at this back in week 4?) It's not an emotional put-down but a call to courage.

> **The assurance of God's presence and His power working on our behalf is why we can be courageous.**

God told Joshua, "Haven't I commanded you: be strong and courageous? Do not be afraid or discouraged, for the LORD your God is with you wherever you go" (Josh. 1:9). The assurance of God's presence and His power working on our behalf is why we can be courageous. Both Elijah and the widow were unable to provide for their own needs. So not only was God inviting the widow into a moment of courageous kindness, but He was asking the same of Elijah.

Go back to the beginning of 1 Kings 17 and read verses 1–7. Before his encounter with the widow, how were Elijah's needs taken care of? How do you think this affected Elijah's faith to believe that a handful of flour and a little bit of oil could be instruments of God's provision?

_____

_____

Now read the rest of 1 Kings 17. List all the ways you see God's kindness at work. What does this tell you about how God can move in and through people who seemingly have nothing to give?

_____

_____

_____

_____

The economy of God is a strange and miraculous thing. The more you give, the more you receive. The more you pour out, the more He fills you up. Elijah was fed by ravens, the widow's final provisions were multiplied beyond reason, and her little boy was brought back to life.

It's no mistake that the name Elijah means "Yahweh is my God." This story is like a flashing neon sign telling every reader of Scripture to remember who God said He is: "Yahweh! The LORD! The God of compassion and mercy! I am slow to anger and filled with unfailing love and faithfulness" (Exod. 34:6 NLT).

It's tempting to read a story like this and focus on the obvious characters. Elijah showed up at the widow's home and asked for a loaf of bread. The widow dipped her hands into the jars of flour and oil and formed the ingredients into loaves. Elijah took the lifeless boy from the widow's arms and cried out to God for his life. Elijah and the widow both showed courage, but they are not the heroes of the story—for it was *God's* power on display!

Friend, living the simple difference and choosing a life of courageous kindness doesn't happen by our own strength but by God's strength in us. We start where we are, give what we have, and God does the rest—more than we could ever expect.

Reread 1 Kings 17:24. What was the widow's conclusion about the miracles she witnessed?

_____

_____

_____

_____

Where in your life is God gently telling you "Do not be afraid" and asking you to trust in His presence, power, and provision?

_____

_____

_____

_____

Reflect on this prayer and make it your own today:

God, thank You for again reminding me that You are compassionate, gracious, slow to anger, and full of lovingkindness. I acknowledge my great need for You. I offer my life—all that I have and all that I am—for Your glory. Use me to show someone else Your kindness this week. Amen.

This is the work of God—that you believe in the one he has sent.

John 6:29

I felt very quiet inside. All the worrying and fear and unknowns in my future had rattled my heart into silence. It was the same kind of eerie silence that sets in after a storm.

I was broke. Actually, my situation was more dire than just being broke. I was in debt. I was in seminary, working as an intern with a local church, and living at my parents' house. My bank account was empty. I wasn't getting a raise anytime soon, my credit cards were maxed out, and my grad school bill was overdue. If I couldn't find seven hundred dollars, I'd have to drop out of school.

Being broke is embarrassing. It's humbling. I felt like I was doing everything I could just to survive. I was serving and loving and counseling high school kids. Every spare moment I had went toward studying and writing papers. Getting a second job wasn't an option. I had exhausted every possibility. The burden felt unbearable. I couldn't fix my way out of this situation. Seven hundred dollars seemed like seven thousand. It was crushing. Unreachable. My impending doom seemed inevitable: I'd have to drop out of grad school and shut down a dream.

In the quiet, I would pray. I didn't even have words—it was more of an exhale. So tired of living in the red, I was scared and felt like such a failure. In that stormy silence, I felt deep sorrow.

Right before I went to unenroll from my spring classes, I made one last stop by my school mailbox. I pulled out my mail. There were a few flyers and a magazine. Underneath the junk mail was a letter addressed to me. I slid my finger down the edge of the envelope and pulled out a single piece of paper. "Dear Anjuli, you have been awarded a scholarship for $1,000."

I sat down completely stunned. I was given *more* money than I had even prayed for. My eyes kept staring at the letter in disbelief. I hadn't applied for this scholarship. I didn't even know it existed. Yet here, at the very moment of my greatest need, God provided. He poured out His provision in abundance. It was a modern-day miracle. There in my grad school lounge, God answered the quiet prayers of my desperate heart.

—ANJULI PASCHALL

When has God answered a desperate prayer or provided for a need in a way you didn't expect?

_____

_____

_____

_____

One of the amazing things about living surrendered to Jesus is receiving the unexpected. We've seen it again and again: Manna sent from heaven. Dinner provided for a ravenous crowd from one boy's small lunch. Blindness becoming clear sight from a mixture of spit and dirt. Ongoing nourishment from oil and flour that were about to run out.

Surprising people with unforeseen acts of kindness seems like one of God's favorite things. Yet there's another common thread to each of these stories: people desperate for God's intervention.

At the very moment Anjuli was on the verge of dropping out of grad school because she couldn't pay her tuition bill, God's kindness was delivered through a seminary mailbox. What are we to conclude from this? Does God not care enough to notice our circumstances until we're in a dire situation? Or perhaps the answer is found in the question we posed yesterday: Is the display of God's power in our lives directly related to acknowledging our desperate need for Him?

God's power gets the spotlight in our times of greatest need.

Indeed, God's power gets the spotlight in our times of greatest need.

Turn to Matthew 4:1–11 and read the story of Jesus's forty days in the wilderness. What *could* Jesus have done in response to His hunger? What did He do instead?

What happened after Jesus endured the trial of temptation (v. 11)? What does this tell you about God's care for His Son?

Jesus had the power to turn those stones into bread. It would have satisfied His intense hunger and shut the mouth of the devil. But instead, Jesus chose to point back to the Father. Jesus modeled what it looks like to put His life in the Father's hands. He trusted that God was sovereign over His circumstances and would ultimately provide for His needs—even if He had to endure trials and suffering along the way.

Through His life and ministry, Jesus continually demonstrated that God is the Giver, the Provider, the Power. Understanding this is crucial for how we interpret our circumstances *and* for how we live surrendered to God.

In earlier weeks, we've looked at the stories of Jesus feeding the five thousand and walking on water. Now let's look at what happened next.

The next day, the crowd was looking for Jesus. When they couldn't locate Him, they went on to Capernaum to continue their search. When they finally found Him, they asked, "What can we do to perform the works of God?" Jesus replied, "This is the work of God—that you believe in the one he has sent" (John 6:28–29).

Read John 6:22–40. What does Jesus first tell the crowd about what they should work for?

Like the crowd, do you ever find yourself longing for the temporary relief of a sign or miracle? But what does verse 40 say God's will is?

It's easy to want the proverbial bread, right? We want God to fix our present predicament, address our immediate crisis or discomfort. Then, when He does, we become anxious for Him to do it again. After the crowd enjoyed the unexpected gift of full bellies, they craved that same satisfied feeling. They saw the evidence of God's power at work through Jesus and His disciples, and they were eager to experience more. But Jesus was warning them to look beyond the temporary relief from hunger (or blindness or a stormy night) and remember that the *who* in their story was far more important than *what* happened.

Anjuli received an unexpected scholarship from her seminary. Amazing grace! But was it the school that really met her need? Only God could have known and orchestrated the impeccable timing of that provision.

The purpose of God's kindness is to draw people to Himself—to be in relationship with Him today and forever. Out of compassion, God addresses our physical needs, which puts His love on display in our lives. No doubt when Anjuli was able to continue with her seminary training and ministry internship, God was using her to reach into the lives of others. His kindness multiplies through our need and our willingness to give from what's been given to us.

Want to live a life of courageous kindness? Want God to use your time, talents, and resources to make a difference? Give Him free reign over everything and believe that He can do more than you ever expected.

Jesus is the bread of life. How is God asking you to believe in Him and to allow Him to satisfy your physical, emotional, or spiritual hunger?

If God's will is that everyone believes in the Son so they can have eternal life, how can living with courageous kindness help accomplish His will?

_____

_____

_____

_____

Reflect on this prayer and make it your own today:

Jesus, thank You for showing me what it looks like to live surrendered to the Father. It's so easy for me to want to strive to meet my own needs and to make a meaningful impact in the lives of others. Yet I don't want to forget that it's all about You. Grow my awareness of how much I need You so that others might be drawn to You through my life. Amen.

Now please swear to me by the LORD that you will also show kindness to my father's family, because I showed kindness to you.

Joshua 2:12

I like to say that my husband Ericlee invested in "community life insurance."

He was the kind of guy who befriended strangers. He would read people's name tags and call them by their first name. Whether we were in the grocery store, bank, airport, inner city, or rural Haiti, he would take time to engage people in conversation.

As a teacher and a coach, Ericlee made meaningful investments in his students and athletes that resulted in lifelong friendships. He pushed people to work hard and chase their dreams. He challenged them to think about issues of faith and held them accountable.

When Ericlee was diagnosed with stage 4 cancer, our mailbox and inboxes overflowed with messages of encouragement and stories of how my husband had influenced lives. Former students, athletes, and friends flocked to our home to pray, sing, and read to him. In all of this, I was lifted and comforted when I needed it most. I knew I was not alone on the journey.

It wasn't until after Ericlee soared to heaven a few months later that I began to more fully understand the power of God's miraculous provision and my husband's courageous kindness.

During his sickness, we had accrued more than $75,000 in medical bills. As a widow raising three young daughters and teaching part-time at the local university, there was no way I could pay those bills on my own. God had other plans.

Some friends from our life group arranged an online auction to help raise money. People from our local community donated gift cards, art items, and getaways at vacation homes. The auction raised several thousand dollars.

One day I received a letter in the mail from a woman I didn't know who had read our story and felt compelled to send us a check. She explained that God was urging her to give. She went to work that day and received an $11,000 bonus. Her husband agreed it was earmarked for us.

Another day I received a fat manila envelope in the mail. When I opened it, cash and checks fell out from people who attended a church in Los Angeles—four hours from where we lived. I didn't know who they were, but I had no doubt they were connected to my husband in some way.

Thousands upon thousands of dollars were donated by friends, churches, strangers, and others in our community who had been touched by Ericlee's life and our story. Every penny of our bills was paid through the generosity of others.

Our insurance did not cover my husband's care but our community did. This was God's miraculous provision for the girls and me. He showed me that He is Immanuel—God with us—through community.

—DORINA LAZO GILMORE-YOUNG

How have you experienced God's kindness through others? Or when have you felt compelled to help someone else in their time of need?

Have you noticed the reciprocal nature of God's kindness? Receiving His love enables us to love others. Loving others compels them to show love in return. Through this, God's love keeps taking center stage—wowing and wooing and drawing people to Him.

Today we're going to look at the story of how one woman's courageous kindness toward two strangers became a catalyst for receiving God's radical kindness.

The woman's name was Rahab, and she was a prostitute whose house was built into the wall that surrounded the city of Jericho. Given her profession, it wasn't odd that she welcomed two men into her home. But when she found out they were Israelite spies who were being hunted by the king of Jericho, she had a choice to make.

Read Joshua 2:1–11. What does Rahab do for the spies? What reason does she give for helping them?

Continue reading verses 12–24. What kindness does Rahab request in return for helping the two men escape?

Conventional wisdom would have told Rahab to trust her own people before trusting outsiders. To seek protection from her king before putting her fate in the hands of the enemy. But Rahab was wise. She allowed the stories she had heard of Yahweh's power to turn her heart to faith instead of fear.

The reality was that if someone saw the spies escaping from her window, surely her own life would be forfeit. Yet Rahab knew her life was safer in the hands of God who is "God in heaven and on earth below" than in her own hands.

So she trusted the oath of the Lord's men because she trusted the Lord. Her faith compelled her to risk her safety for the sake of protecting others. She chose courageous kindness to honor God, no matter the cost.

Read Joshua 6. What happened when the Israelites attacked Jericho? Did God make good on His promise to Rahab?

_____

_____

_____

_____

Imagine what it would have been like to be surrounded by Israel's army. What do you think was going through Rahab's mind as she heard the troops shouting and the trumpets blaring and the mighty city wall around her home crumbling?

_____

_____

_____

_____

_____

Rahab demonstrated nothing short of tremendous courage. First by hiding two enemy spies on her roof, negotiating a deal with them, devising a plan for their safe escape, and helping them get away through her window undetected. Then, when the city was under siege, by gathering her family and tying that scarlet cord in her window. She waited for God's deliverance even when the circumstances looked grim.

Rahab's life shows that the faith and kindness of one woman matters. Not only did her actions have lasting implications for her family— you know, being saved from total annihilation and all—but God also used her story as an example for all generations. Her courageous obedience is recorded in Hebrews 11 among a long list of faith heroes: "By faith Rahab the prostitute welcomed the spies in peace and didn't perish with those who disobeyed" (v. 31). Her legacy is mentioned again in James 2:25 in a discussion about the importance of faith and actions working together.

One act of courageous kindness—by a woman whose worth was discounted—was like a single stone with many ripples.

Our opening story showed the same thing. Dorina's late husband, Ericlee, lived a life marked by courageous kindness. Though his days were cut shorter than anyone would have hoped, his legacy of kindness created waves of lasting change for his wife and three young daughters. His faith in God and love for others became a catalyst for kindness from friends and strangers alike.

> **One act of courageous kindness is like a single stone with many ripples.**

Kindness begets kindness. Love begets love. Keep reminding yourself that this is the wild economy of God.

Read James 2:14–26. What is the relationship between what we believe and what we do?

If faith without works is dead, how can living with courageous kindness breathe fresh life into your faith? What one step of faith in action is God asking you to take this week?

Reflect on this prayer and make it your own today:

God, thank You that when the world tells me I have to take care of myself, You call me to trust in You. Because of Your goodness and mercy, I know that I can love others well, even when it's costly. Please give me courage today to show Your kindness to someone in need, and build my faith to trust that Your kindness will also be at work in my life. Amen.

Your beauty and love chase after me every day of my
life.

Psalm 23:6 MSG

I pull into a parking spot at Aldi, then search the change
compartment in our van so I can pay the shopping cart
fee. There are no quarters. I berate myself in silence.

Why am I so bad at grocery shopping, keeping lists, and maintaining routines? If I just got my act together, surely things would be better for everyone. I should be better by now, more like every other mom I know. What is wrong with me?

I find a Canadian dollar coin between a stack of pennies and nickels
and decide to try to stuff it into the slot where quarters are supposed to
go. I think about my empty fridge at home and pray it works.

As I approach the row of locked carts, a man is coming toward
me from the opposite direction to return his cart. I slow my pace, not
wanting him to see me attempt to shove the wrong coin into the slot,
but he passes the cart return and keeps heading toward me. He offers
me his cart. Before I try to awkwardly offer him my Canadian dollar
and hope he has a trip to Canada in the works, he says, "I don't need
the quarter."

It's the tiniest gesture. It's the quickest exchange. I almost start
crying as I stand there in the August afternoon heat, sweating and
clutching my imposter coin.

It wasn't just that things had worked out. It was the image of God I saw in that unsuspecting man. It was the tenderness and nearness of God I felt in a twenty-five-cent detail.

The stranger offered me a cart and a quarter, and I received much more than that. He didn't know that his kindness pushed back the darkness of my own self-hate, my lack of grace, and this phantom woman I carried around in my back pocket and compared myself to. His tiny offering became something powerful: the love and kindness of God meeting me and fighting for me on the hot, black, everyday surface of a grocery store parking lot.

—TASHA JUN

When has God reminded you of His love through a small act of kindness from a stranger? What effect did that have on your day or maybe even your life?

Could the drumbeat of God's heart for you be any louder? *Kindness. Kind-ness. Kind-ness.* Hear the rhythm of His love pounding out through strangers and quarters, Jesus Christ and the living Word. Even sweaty August afternoons with frustrating errands can become a melody of God's relentless love and care.

At some point, we all need a fresh reminder that there's no valley too dark or pit too deep for God's redemptive love and steadfast compassion to reach us. In times like that, the book of Psalms is the perfect place to turn. The psalms are songs of anguish and songs of praise—and every one of them sings of God's heart for His people.

Today we're going to look at Psalm 23, which you might be familiar with already. But because God's Word is alive and active, we can trust that He has fresh and timely encouragement.

Let the opening lines wash over you like an invitation:

> The LORD is my shepherd;
> I have what I need.
> He lets me lie down in green pastures;
> he leads me beside quiet waters. (vv. 1–2)

Read all of Psalm 23. Remember that God's name Yahweh is translated in our English Bibles as "the LORD." Taking what you've learned so far about Yahweh, how does this psalm support who God says He is? (Refer back to Exodus 34:5–7 if needed.)

_____

_____

_____

_____

What verses from Psalm 23 do you long to be true in your own life today? Which words or promises are hard for you to believe today?

_____

_____

_____

_____

This psalm was written by David. Before slaying the famous giant Goliath (which we'll talk about tomorrow), before becoming a hunted fugitive or the king of Israel, David was a shepherd. He had intimate knowledge about the relationship between a flock and its leader. He knew firsthand how desperate sheep are for guidance and protection, and he knew the powerful influence of a good shepherd.

So when David says, "The LORD is my shepherd," he's making a bold declaration about his own neediness as well as God's goodness and trustworthiness. David acknowledges that with God as his shepherd, all his needs will be provided for. That doesn't mean he will never encounter rocky terrain or times of drought; it doesn't mean predators won't still prowl and trials won't still come—but David knows He is not alone in facing them.

When we declare God as our shepherd, we are not alone either.

What has been your darkest valley? Looking back (or maybe you're there now), how can you see that God was with you? What do you think it means that "his rod and staff" are a source of comfort?

Read Ezekiel 34:11–16. How do God's words about Himself and how He pursues His people line up with how David describes his relationship with God in Psalm 23?

So much of life feels like a big question mark. Which way should you go? What job should you take? Who should you marry? What kind of friend should you make? In every ordinary day, we make thousands of decisions. The man in the Aldi parking lot had to decide whether to return his cart or keep pushing toward the stranger.

The volume and weight of the questions and decisions we face can be overwhelming. Yet over and over Scripture promises that God will guide us. Here in Psalm 23 it says, "He leads me along the right paths" (v. 3). This is good and true and packs a powerful punch of hope. But just as important as *what* God does for us is *why* He does it.

The whole of verse 3 says, "He renews my life; he leads me along the right paths *for his name's sake*." Or as the New Living Translation puts it, "He renews my strength. He guides me along right paths, *bringing honor to his name*."

It's time to rehearse the truth from the beginning of this week: *It's not about us!* God loves His kids and delights in giving good gifts—that's who He is! We follow God's lead—whether in green pastures or Aldi parking lots—so that *He* can get the glory.

> **We follow God's lead so that *He* can get the glory.**

So that His name flashes bright on the marquee of our lives.

And others will read all about Him.

Open your Bible app or go to BibleGateway.com and read Psalm 23:6 in a few different translations. What do words like *follow*, *pursue*, or *chase after* tell you about God's kindness?

Think about how God's love and goodness have been evident in your life recently. How does this spur you on in your commitment to live with courageous kindness?

_____

_____

_____

_____

Reflect on this prayer and make it your own today:

Lord, You are my shepherd. Thank You for offering me comfort and refreshment when I'm weary and frazzled. Thank You for leading me when I'm prone to lose my way, for guiding me when I'm likely to stumble or stray. Open my eyes today to the reality of Your active protection and provision in my life, and then use me as a conduit of kindness—for Your name's sake. Amen.

Let the favor of the LORD our God be on us;
establish for us the work of our hands—
establish the work of our hands!

Psalm 90:17

When COVID-19 began spreading and our school district decided it was safer for students to engage in virtual school from home for a while, my first priority was creating a new routine for our family. I sat down with my daughters to let them know my plans and expectations, and I explained that we'd be adding some new habits to our days. In addition to vigorously cleaning all our frequently touched surfaces and completing our work at the dining room table each morning, we would begin sending notes or cards to our family and friends once a week.

At first everyone thought this was great fun. We all missed seeing our favorite people in person, so sending a note, a card, or a page from a coloring book was an outlet for those feelings. But as the weeks went on, with us sending a little stack of mail each Monday yet rarely finding anything in our own mailbox, one of my daughters expressed her disappointment.

"Why doesn't anyone send *us* a letter in the mail? Why are we even doing this?"

I understood her frustration. After all, how many times have I lamented the fact that I always seem to be the friend who initiates time together? It hurts when we feel like affection or encouragement is a one-way street. Both my daughter and I needed a new perspective on our "Mail Mondays."

I told her (and reminded myself) that we weren't sending our friends and family notes or cards in order to get something in return. We were doing it simply to show them how much we loved them and to encourage them during this especially difficult time.

A few days after that conversation, I was on the phone with my friend who is also our pastor's wife. As we wrapped up our call, she said, "Oh, Mary! I wanted to tell you . . ." She went on to tell me that the note I'd sent our pastor the week before came at exactly the right moment. She shared that he'd been feeling overwhelmed with all that comes with pastoring during a pandemic, and my note of appreciation and encouragement made a big difference for him and for their family.

Tears filled my eyes and all I could think to say was how grateful I was that God had used a little kindness and a stamp to make such a big difference. I'd had no idea our pastor was struggling; I just knew that sending a word of encouragement was one small way I could show God's love to my friends and family—even if they never wrote me back.

—MARY CARVER

Have you ever grown weary of doing good or doubted that a small act of kindness really mattered? How important are our perspective and expectations when it comes to showing kindness?

For six weeks we've been learning what it means to be women of courageous kindness. Let's close with one more powerful example of how something small can make a big impact when we have the courage to show up and believe God can accomplish His purpose through us.

You're probably familiar with the story of David and Goliath, found in 1 Samuel 17. Here's a quick refresher. Goliath was a nearly ten-foot-tall Philistine warrior who threatened to destroy the Israelite army. Day after day for forty days, Goliath came forward and challenged any man from the opposing side who was brave enough to face him. The future of both peoples rested on this single man-to-man combat. Whichever side was victorious would lay claim to their enemy's land, wealth, and citizens. Saul was king of Israel, and not one soldier in his mighty legion was willing to fight such a powerful opponent with everything on the line.

The Israelites were woefully aware of their own insufficiency, but they failed to understand that God's power was what they really needed. Enter David. At this time, David was a teenage shepherd, the youngest of eight sons. His father sent him to the battlefield with provisions for his brothers. When David got to the front lines and heard about the dire situation his people faced, he didn't hesitate to offer his help.

Read 1 Samuel 17:20–37. What do you think made the young shepherd willing to fight an opponent that hundreds of trained soldiers wouldn't face? Was David simply conceited, like his older brother suggested?

_____

_____

_____

_____

How does recalling what God had done for him in the past help David to have courage and confidence for the future?

David's uncanny courage came from knowing that it would be God's power—not his own—that would defeat the giant. He was simply willing to be the conduit.

David approached the Philistine with nothing but a sling and a pouch full of river rocks. He took one smooth stone, placed it in his sling, and let it fly. The rock sank into the Philistine's forehead, taking down the seemingly unconquerable foe.

Just picture it: a sheep-tending boy standing on the battlefield, demonstrating God's undeniable power.

So what does an old Bible story that reads like a mythic fairy tale have to do with being women of courageous kindness today? While it's unlikely that we will ever be asked to defeat an entire army by slaying an epic giant, each of us is sure to encounter opportunities to make a difference when the odds are stacked against us. Most certainly we will see someone in need—today in our neighborhood or tomorrow at work or next week at church—and look down at our own measly stones and sling and be tempted to think, *It's impossible for someone like me to make a difference.*

The correct response? Yes, it is impossible . . . without God. But with God, all things are possible.

Continue reading 1 Samuel 17:38–58 and see for yourself how God used one small stone to create a tidal wave of change. Is there any

evidence that David had control over the outcome? What does David identify as his most powerful weapon?

Read Luke 18:27 and write down what Jesus said. While Jesus is talking specifically about salvation, how can you see the truth of His words play out in David's life and in your own?

In our opening story, Mary and her young daughters were trying to thrive (or just survive) during a global pandemic and had a desire to make an impact beyond the confines of their home. There were a lot of things they couldn't do at that time, but Mary focused on what they *could* do—give the small gift of encouragement through ink and crayons and a stamped envelope.

Was Mary responsible for the outcome of each note? Could she control whether their Monday Mail would be reciprocated or make a difference in the lives of the recipients? Nope. But she could rally her daughters and faithfully offer their simple act of kindness.

In the same way, David wasn't responsible for how his battle against Goliath went down. But he was responsible for hearing God, responding in faith, and showing up. An entire nation of people was changed because of it.

We live with courage and kindness so God can shine through us.

We live with courage and kindness not so we can garner fame or approval but so God can shine through us and do more than we could ever expect.

We offer our pebble. God's power magnifies the ripples. He accomplishes with a stone what we cannot do on our own.

Look up Ephesians 3:14–21. Read it slowly. Let it wash over you like a promise. Write down your response to God.

_____

_____

_____

_____

Read Psalm 90:17 as a courageous kindness anthem. How is God asking you to trust in His power and partner with Him in the work of courageous kindness today?

_____

_____

_____

_____

_____

Reflect on this prayer and make it your own today:

Yahweh—my Father, my Savior, Holy Spirit—thank You for choosing to put Your power and purpose to work in my life. I recognize that You have called me to live with a posture of courageous kindness so that Your kindness can increase. I trust You with my small stones. Take the little I have and multiply it. I believe You can and will do immeasurably more than anything I could ask or imagine. I am Yours. Amen.

> ▶ **For a deeper look at this week's study and to spur on discussion if you're working with a small group, watch a FREE video from (in)courage at incourage.me/biblestudy.**

notes

Week 1   Right Where You Are

1. *Thayer's Greek Lexicon*, s.v. "Strong's NT 342: ἀνακαίνωσις [*anakainósis*]," https://biblehub.com/greek/342.htm.
2. John Mark Comer, *God Has a Name* (Grand Rapids: Zondervan, 2017), 42.
3. Johannes P. Louw and Eugene Albert Nida, *Greek-English Lexicon of the New Testament: Based on Semantic Domains* (New York: United Bible Societies, 1996), 369.
4. *Strong's Exhaustive Concordance*, s.v. "*pisteuó*," https://biblehub.com/strongs/greek/4100.htm.
5. *Strong's Concordance*, s.v. "*agathos*," https://biblehub.com/greek/18.htm.

Week 2   Exactly What You Have

1. Ken Gire, *Moments with the Savior* (Grand Rapids: Zondervan, 1998), 276–77.

Week 3   Bending Low and Lifting Up

1. Jodi Hooper, "Jesus Heals the Paralyzed Man," Bible.org, June 25, 2012, https://bible.org/seriespage/6-jesus-heals-paralyzed-man-matthew-91-8-mark-21-12.

Week 4   Compassion and Inconvenience

1. Stephen D. Renn, *Expository Dictionary of Bible Words: Word Studies for Key English Bible Words Based on the Hebrew and Greek Texts* (Peabody, MA: Hendrickson, 2005), 672.
2. Darrel L. Bock, *Luke*, NIV Application Commentary (Grand Rapids: Zondervan, 1996), 300.
3. *Ellicott's Commentary for English Readers*, https://biblehub.com/commentaries/1_peter/4-10.htm.

about the authors

Becky Keife is the (in)courage community manager. She is a speaker and the author of *The Simple Difference* and *No Better Mom for the Job*. Becky is a big fan of Sunday naps and championing women. She lives near Los Angeles and loves hiking shady trails with her husband and three spirited sons. Find her at beckykeife.com and on Instagram @beckykeife.

Karina Allen is devoted to helping women live out their unique calling and building authentic community through practical application of Scripture in an approachable, winsome manner. Connect with her on Instagram @karina268.

Stephanie Bryant is the cofounder of (in)courage and host of the *Jesus Led Adventure* podcast. She's passionate about guiding women into their promised land, and enjoys spending her days with her husband and their miracle daughter on their farm. Find Stephanie at stephaniebryant.me and on Instagram @StephanieSBryant.

Mary Carver is a writer and speaker who lives for good books, spicy queso, and television marathons—but lives because of God's grace. She writes about giving up on perfect and finding truth in unexpected places at MaryCarver.com and on Instagram @marycarver. Mary and her husband live in Kansas City with their two daughters.

Grace P. Cho is the (in)courage editorial manager. In the middle of her years in church ministry, she sensed God moving her toward writing, to use her words to lead. She coaches writers, mentors leaders, and believes that telling our stories can change the world. Connect with her on Instagram @gracepcho.

Robin Dance is the author of *For All Who Wander*, is married to her college sweetheart, and is as Southern as sugar-shocked tea. An empty nester with a full life, she's determined to age with grace and laugh at the days to come. Connect with her at robindance.me and on Instagram @robindance.me.

Dorina Lazo Gilmore-Young is a multicultural speaker, Bible teacher, foodie, mentor, and trail runner, and author of the devotional *Walk, Run, Soar*. She helps people navigate grief and chase after God's glory. Dorina and her husband, Shawn, are raising three brave girls in central California. Find her at dorinagilmore.com and on Instagram @dorinagilmore.

Tasha Jun is a melancholy dreamer, a Korean girl, wife to Matt, and mama to three little warriors. She loves French fries, spicy soup, and wandering the world. Tasha's always lived in places where cultures collide, longing for home. Jesus found her and has been leading her toward wholeness and home ever since. Find her on Instagram @tashajunb and at tashajun.com.

Aliza Latta is a Canadian writer, journalist, and artist, who is a huge fan of telling stories. She writes about faith and young adulthood at alizalatta.com, and is the author of the novel *Come Find Me, Sage Parker*. Find her on Instagram @alizalatta.

Anjuli Paschall is a pastor's wife, spiritual director, writer, and mom to five kids. She is the author of *Stay: Discovering Grace, Freedom, and Wholeness Where You Never Imagined Looking*. Anjuli writes daily on Instagram @lovealways.anjuli and is the founder of @TheMomsWeLoveClub.

Anna E. Rendell is the (in)courage digital content manager and lives in Minnesota with her husband and four kids. She loves a good book and a great latte. Anna is the author of *Pumpkin Spice for Your Soul* and *A Moment of Christmas*. Visit her at AnnaRendell.com and on Instagram @annaerendell.

Bible Studies to Refresh Your Soul

In these six-week Bible studies, your friends at (in)courage will help you dive deep into real-life issues, the transforming power of God's Word, and what it means to courageously live your faith.

100 Days of Hope and Peace

In this 100-day devotional, the (in)courage community reaches into the grief and pain of both crisis and ordinary life. Each day includes a key Scripture, a heartening devotion, and a prayer to remind you that God is near and hope is possible. You won't find tidy bows or trite quick fixes, just arrows pointing you straight to Jesus.

(in)

(in)courage welcomes you

to a place where authentic, brave women connect deeply with God and others. Through the power of shared stories and meaningful resources, (in)courage champions women and celebrates the strength Jesus gives to live out our calling as God's daughters. Together we build community, celebrate diversity, and **become women of courage**.

Join us at **www.incourage.me**
& connect with us on social media!